"Neal Grace's *Fresh Eyes Upon The World* is a brilliant manual. Comprehensive in scope, it covers art, nature, diet, music, the environment, relationships, animals and much more. His book is exceptionally well written and is never unnecessarily complicated. By covering such a wide range of topics, Neal makes it possible for everyone to relate to his book and as a result, the world is blessed for it. A magnificent work of literature by a modern-day sage. Bravo!"

Mazdak Khamda, Music teacher,
Dominican University.

"This little gem of a book prompts us to ask the questions that lead to a conscious life. It challenges us to think about the big questions. Covering each topic in just two or three pages, the book kick-starts our ability to scrutinize our assumptions and catalyze fresh thinking. As you use Neal's wisdom to illuminate your own journey, you'll find yourself thinking more deeply about every aspect of your life and the planet we share together. This wonderful book will leave you enriched and more aware of the potential that a consciously lived life represents."

Dawson Church, PhD,
author of the award-winning science book
*Mind To Matter: The Astonishing Science
Of How Your Brain Creates Material Reality.*

Fresh Eyes
Upon the World
Making Life A Spectacular Journey

NEAL GRACE

GRIZZLY PEAK PRESS
Kensington, California

For information contact:

Grizzly Peak Press
350 Berkeley Park Boulevard
Kensington, California 94707
grizzlypeakpress.com

Design, layout and typesetting by
Liquid Pictures
www.liquidpictures.com

Original Cover Photo by Zachary Rymland

ISBN Number: 978-0-9988310-4-6
Library of Congress Number: 2018946286

Printed in the United States of America

COMPASSION

One gentle nudge, one tender gaze,
One word of encouragement
Can lift a fallen soul from sadness
To a life of happiness!

Neal Grace

AUTHOR'S NOTE

From the moment we are conceived, we begin a ceaseless journey of change that forms who we are. Many factors influence and shape our identities. We do our best to function well in a world full of tumult and challenges. Survival for most of us presents some daunting tasks we must resolve before we can move on to the next plateau of our destiny. Life for us humans is full of sublime experiences and terrifying fears.

We do, however, control more of our lives than we realize. Oftentimes, we feel like a victim to the rough and unpredictable tides of life. We feel tossed around by waves over which we have no control. These feelings can be effectively managed once we gain a command of ourselves.

Life is synonymous with self-discovery. We are always learning about who we are. But this process requires some serious soul searching. We need to sort out all the threads of our previous experiences in order to weave a smooth tapestry of who we want to be in this world.

In this book, I have compiled many relevant questions for you to think about and to explore. The answers are intended to inspire you to reflect upon your own life to see how they impact you.

I strongly believe that the only way we as individuals can liberate ourselves from delusions, fear and prejudice is to embark upon a passionate journey of self-examination. Society can heal and transform its darkness only when each of us develops holistic, compassionate and humanitarian core values that will lead to a happier, more fulfilled existence. Our future survival rests with us. Civilization will thrive as we champion the virtues that can make life safer and more beautiful for all of us!

Neal Grace

Fresh Eyes
Upon The World

CONTENTS

Section Two   **104**

Hotly Debated Issues

Section Three   **158**

The World & Nature

Section Four   *187*

Spirituality & Philosophy

Section Five   **234**

Other Subjects

Fresh Eyes
Upon The World

SECTION ONE

Self-Empowerment &
Relationships

Nothing is more important to a person than self-discovery. Each of us is learning more about who we are, and the miracles of which we are made, every day. This discovery process leads us closer to the place within us where we can feel more alive and in alignment with others and the world. The questions and answers in this section act as potent catalysts to push us closer to the truth about human life, teaching us how to empower ourselves to live a more meaningful and purposeful existence.

1.

How Can I Be More Receptive To New Ideas?

Live everyday as a wondrous adventure by being open to new ideas.

Most of us stay within the boundaries of the status quo because they are familiar, safe and controllable. The human mind has a vast potential of ideas, most of which get shot down by the ego's fear of newness. Growth and change are essential to our personal wellbeing. Information comes to us in a variety of ways. It is true, we have a tendency to defend what we think is the correct way. We get stale and rigid, clinging tightly to our beliefs, forcing the past to overshadow the newness of the present.

One of the best ways to become more receptive to new ideas is to sit back, allowing them to come to you in a neutral frame of mind. Don't prematurely jump to conclusions about these ideas. Say to yourself how fortunate you are to be given them. Sift through them slowly, savor them, ruminate upon them, and then try them on to see if they enhance your life. Develop the muscle in your mind that says: "I embrace this idea with enthusiasm. I will add it as another item to my repertoire that has guided me successfully to this present moment. I will try this new thought to see how it will work in my life."

Be adventurous; be willing to try something new and fresh. I know many people who refuse to go to new restaurants. They don't want to try something different. They are not receptive to new foods. This lack of receptivity prevents them from experiencing a type of food which they might totally love. You have to experiment with new things in order to see if they work for you. Ideas are like books you have never read. Once you read them, you can decide what you want to remember as kernels of wisdom that will strengthen your life as you continue on your journey. You don't have to accept everything new that is presented to you. But at least be willing to closely examine these ideas to see if they have validity and purpose.

2.

How Can I Come From My Higher Self And Love All People?

Treat everyone as if he or she were your friend!

What you can do, by coming from your highest self, is to appreciate people. Be kind to them. Don't judge them; don't be disapproving; don't be insensitive to them. Treat them with respect, even if you can't understand their lifestyle or their values. Everyone is trying to do his or her best, trying to survive and trying to find love in the vast world. Open your heart to people; smile at them; offer them an uplifting thought; encourage them. A simple suggestion can go a long way. Offer them your love in the

24

smallest gestures. This is the way to love the people of this planet. Nod at a stranger passing you in the street; offer to help a disabled person; help a blind person to his destination. Be a shining light to yourself and the whole world will be a little brighter and a little happier.

When you make peace with the vast variety of people on Earth, your experience of life brightens and you feel safer and more relaxed. Most of us want to be loved, but we forget how to give love because we are worried about rejection. Open your heart to other people; they cannot hurt you or disappoint you unless you allow them to do this. Trust in the goodness of human nature. Despite all the underpinnings and discord in the world, people want to be loved and cherished. Make people your friends who will support you and inspire you as you make your way into the unknown mystery of tomorrow.

3.

What Inspires Creativity
In People?

*Within each of us is the potential for
extraordinary creativity!*

The irrepressible urge to discover the beauty living inside all of us propels individuals to express themselves in original, creative ways. This beauty is also called love for life, love for the journey of the human experience. A person takes the physical properties existing on the outside and begins to mix them with the blend of his or her own ingredients of understanding the mystery of the world.

People are inspired because there is energy within all of us that wants to be expressed in unique and artistic ways. It is easy to be inspired since we are all searching for a deeper meaning to our existence. Creativity enables us to experience this meaning. It brings our feelings, dreams, hopes and love into material forms for us to cherish and to share with other people.

Being creative is like giving birth to something alive and wondrous gestating within our souls. There is no way to stop this creativity from expressing itself. It is the nature of life to continuously recreate itself. Creativity is also a new language containing cryptic messages of who we are. It is a more precise and more all-encompassing way of revealing our true nature than all the words in the world can convey. Another reason behind the inspiration of creativity is that it gives the person a direct experience of the sacredness of life. It allows us to feel the power of creation itself in the small but miraculous manifestation of creativity.

4.

What Is The Secret Formula High Achievers Use To Motivate Themselves To Become Successful?

The magic formula for success is revamping our core beliefs.

Most people think high achievers come from a special ilk and possess a seminal, built-in drive giving them the right ingredients to be successful. This is not true. The people who reach summits of success share a common denominator, which is available to anyone. What they own is an unrelenting determination to reach their goals no matter what the conditions look like on the outside. In other words, they are unstoppable in their pursuit of a dream. They may become discouraged at times, but nothing rips their drive from them. They want to succeed so passionately their energy propels them onward, as if by some mystical force. This high level fuel or motivation is available to all of us.

You just need an inner confidence unmarred and unscathed by all the naysayers who emphatically denounce you or tell you your dream is totally implausible. You need to love the process leading to success, not stopping along the way to count your losses or wallow in the disappointment at how long it is taking to get you where you want to go. There is a fire burning inside the high achiever which cannot be squelched even by a torrent of water! If you can believe in yourself without being conceited—and embrace a strong sense of humility—you can do anything in this world.

How does an ordinary person incorporate this major attitudinal change into his or her life? Simply by shifting the understanding from an external one to an internal one. The external one thrives on getting positive feedback from outside sources. This is not a bad thing, but you cannot rely on others to keep you buoyed as you follow your dream. The outside is not the source of your strength—you are! The internal one taps into a deep reservoir inside you that offers you its ample power and enthusiasm as long as you allow it to flow without blocking it with your doubts, fears, reticence, and apprehension.

Believe in yourself. Feel great about who you are and how you live. If you question whether you are worthy of stupendous success or deserve it, you will smash your chances to smithereens. You need undeviating focus, trust, hope, and gratitude as you climb the mountain alone to reach the summit of your most impassioned dream.

5.

What Is The Best Way To Heal Loneliness?

Healing loneliness begins with how you perceive yourself—not how others see you.

Loneliness afflicts people for short bursts of time almost every day we live. Let me define loneliness before I offer solutions how to combat it. Loneliness is when you feel out of sorts with yourself. It is when you feel estranged from other people and no one knows you and you cannot communicate the depth of your feelings to anyone. You feel marooned on a deserted island with no way of escaping. It is a tragic feeling that engulfs you in a palpable suffering where breathing becomes difficult. It is so overpowering it can suffocate you. It breaks the flow of life. It pulls you away from the tides and mires you in a death-like quicksand pulling you under.

Loneliness is when you have lost your confidence and your power. You feel helpless to reach out to others. When you do you can't seem to connect well. You are left bereft of hope. The world turns acrid, parched like a burnt forest. Nothing can save you because your loneliness is self-induced. That's right—this horrible feeling has been brought on by your own inner despair about yourself. You feel alienated from everyone around you. This entire feeling was born inside your mind, which decided you are a failure. You blame yourself and then begin to spiral downward into a self-loathing nightmare where loneliness begins to consume you.

Healing loneliness is probably one of the greatest challenges to a person. Everyone you encounter is a blur to you because your fear of loneliness accentuates the inability to connect. People think being around another person and sharing with him will alleviate the symptoms of loneliness. This will only temporarily dispel the feelings. It will not remove them. Once the person is gone, you are left again with a flood of loneliness sweeping over you.

Keeping loneliness in check demands a thorough self-purging. You must remove the cobwebs of your self-doubt and self-deprecating energies. You cannot blame anything on the outside. Other people have not made you feel lonely. You have made yourself feel this way. You have, on some obscure level, chosen to be miserable in a state of loneliness. You have judged yourself unworthy of genuine affections from other people and from yourself.

You are always alone and no other person or thousands of people can banish your solitary journey through life. You are your own separate planet sailing in a galaxy of billions of other planets! Accept this. Honor this. Own this. Then you will be able to invite others to enter your world because the clouds of fear will dissipate, leaving a clear space for someone to discover you. You will find peace in your aloneness and will also enjoy the company of another. You will not demand the other person serve you to quell your loneliness. You will serve yourself with the delightful pleasure of a self-acceptance so profound radiance will emanate from your soul.

There are millions of people around you who also want to connect with others. Reach out to them. Show them who you are. Take the initiative to introduce them to your best friend—you! If they don't want to play with you or don't understand you, smile and let them go their way without you. Wish them well. You will be left with yourself.

This is a divine gift. You came into the world alone and you will leave the world alone. You have yourself. You have the spirit of life with you at all times. You have a billion sisters and brothers around you who are looking to link arms with you to march together toward the sunset!

6.

How Can I Be My Authentic Self?

The more you trust yourself and trust the world, the freer and more genuine you will become.

This is a question of great importance that most people seldom ask. Most people think they are living from their authentic, intrinsic nature. They are not. It is a profound journey of introspection and self-inquiry of the most intensive kind to discover who you are. Being authentic takes courage, strength and self-knowledge that happen gradually over time. You need to examine your motives and your beliefs leading to your actions to ascertain the truth about yourself.

We all wear subtle masks when interacting with other people. Most of the time, we are not conscious of these masks. We wear them because we have learned over time how to successfully engage with people by saying the correct things, thinking the accepted beliefs and believing the right things. What's missing is objective examination of the origins of our actions. Where did the thoughts come from and why are we attached to them. We have failed to question the process that pounded ideas and behavior into our beings.

Being authentic means you must discover who you are and choose to live this life at all costs. You must sort out your values, beliefs and perceptions of the world to decide which ones truly reflect who you are. The conditioning process, which has followed us our entire lives, is extremely difficult to shake. We were molded by positive and negative reinforcement from the moment of our birth. The only way to peel away the thousands of layers of conditioning is to become aware of them one at a time. We often emulate the behavioral traits of our parents without realizing it. This is not natural. We are an amalgamation of various parts of other people as well.

To become your natural, authentic self is to be conscious of who you want to be and what feels most comfortable to you. It requires tremendous concentration to step outside of a role society has deemed acceptable. Many people act as stereotypes cast from some superficial die. Their language seems contrived and artificial; even the way they conduct themselves, with little mannerisms, seems forced and unnatural. It is because they have lost consciousness about themselves. They have assumed a role that, with lots of repetition, feels as though it is who they really are. It is not.

The path to freedom and authenticity is a conscious one you must act upon by identifying the energy, passion, ideas, values and beliefs—living within you—that are tethered to the fixed position of a social structure demanding your conformity. Step outside of the comfort zone to see what's there. Step beyond the limits you have placed upon yourself to find the wings waiting to be unfurled, so you can learn to fly. Don't rebel just to be different. Don't be a maverick just to poke at the conventions of the accepted norm. Don't be an iconoclast just for the sake of ruffling other's feathers. Don't be anything except who you decide you are. Then live it without encumbrance. Live it so gloriously you taste freedom in every moment of your life.

7

Why Do People Join Cults And Gangs?

We can help others to find balance in their lives with the power of our compassion.

cceptance. The need for family is so powerful that people without a place, where they feel loved and appreciated, will seek desperate alternatives. Once a person is ostracized from school, family, or the neighborhood, he or she will implode with resentment. Reeling from this intense rejection, he will find a group of individuals who will accept him. Then the group thinking takes over his personality and he fights furiously to keep the group thriving because without it to support him, he will be tossed into a painful alienation that will drain the life force from him. This is why gangs have such a fanatical fear of other gangs. They have become so exclusive and protective of their own survival, everything else is perceived as a vicious threat that needs to be kept in check.

Cults operate with a similar premise. The only thing that matters is to perpetuate the organization by viewing everything outside with suspicion. Cults use religious dogma to keep their members in abeyance and complacent. Never question the organization, for to do so is to commit heresy and thus risk being thrown back into the cold, unloving world to fend for yourself. Cults become a vicarious family where extreme loyalty is not only expected but demanded. Once a person has been properly indoctrinated into a cult, it is almost impossible to remove him from it. The need to belong in human nature is so powerful, people will do almost anything to feel a part of a family of like-minded individuals.

The best way to keep young people out of cults and gangs is to offer a nurturing environment where love is pervasive. Be understanding and empathic; be aware of their feelings; be keenly observant to see how they are adjusting to the world. Talk to them. Open your heart to them. The pain of separation and alienation is so incalculable to a human soul its impact can never be underestimated. Become a friend to a person struggling to fit in and you will have given a precious gift by encouraging him on his journey to find himself in the midst of a complicated, sometimes unwelcoming society. Your kindness to this person will stay with him the rest of his life. Become a beacon of light leading him to a gentle place he can call home.

8.

When There Is A Lot Of Drudgery In The World, How Can I Feel More Alive?

Life is a continuous stream of exciting opportunities waiting for us to discover them!

Plunge through a hole in a frozen lake! Seriously, most people feel weighed down by a lackluster energy, a form of lethargy that casts a pall over them. It is common in the West to think your life is stagnating. It makes you feel morose and downtrodden; you become jaded as you move sluggishly through the activities of the day. The cause of this comes from the mind, the place where negative attitudes get piled up like logs stuck in a narrow opening. With time, the energy flow becomes restricted and you feel as though you've been injected with a powerful tranquilizer.

There is an easy way out of this drudgery. Wake up from the dream you have been living in black and white, choosing to now see everything in lustrous color. It's as simple as that: Shift your attitude, put on new lenses, remove the heavy cloak you have been wearing and then take a good look at the world around you.

There will never be a second in your life where you will not experience astounding amazement! Look at a leaf! Look deeply until tears form in your eyes at witnessing a thing as miraculous as a leaf. Look at a pebble. Keep absorbing it into your being. It is an ossified piece of early Earth. Its beauty is immeasurable. Follow the flight of a sparrow and feel your heart racing with joy at such blissful mobility. Eat a fresh strawberry and feel your taste buds quiver in ecstasy. Breathe in the scented air of an evergreen forest and tell me your entire body doesn't shudder at such a life-affirming event? Look at the waves of the ocean and you will fall down in sheer wonder at such a hypnotic dance of a living miracle.

Keep going. Never stop. Keep immersing yourself into everything with the unfettered excitement of a child, and you will go crazy with yourself. Look at a turtle; a crow;

a snake; a kitten; a cow and you will see the perfection of eons before you. Listen to thunder and tremble at its power. Listen to a harp and feel yourself being swept into a euphoric state you never knew possible. Listen to your own voice; its vibration; its volume; its melody—and you will know the mystery of the spirit inside you.

Touch another hand! It is amazing, this other living creature sharing the same world as you! Kiss a person whom you love! Have you fainted yet from the intense pleasure of connecting in the harmonic song of love? Are you enraptured yet?

Take a shower! My goodness, it feels like a piece of divinity! Walk under a full moon and listen to the crickets! Are you dreaming yet? Watch dancers on stage and behold the elegance, grace and strength of these lithe bodies performing feats beyond belief.

Swim in the sea, dive into the waves, slide across a frozen pond, ski, and ride a bicycle along a stream.

Climb a verdant hill until you reach the summit and then gaze out in all directions with the wind in your hair. Is there anything in the vast panorama that is misplaced and doesn't belong there? Watch nimbus clouds drifting above your head. Are you smiling yet? Do you feel a magic rippling throughout your body?

Paddle a kayak by yourself in the dawn of a summer day in a mountain lake. Is the serenity of this moment purer than all the fantasies you have ever conceived?

Shall I list some mundane things? Are these any less sensational than the agreed upon monumental things? The taste of cool water; a smile from a little girl; a drink of mango juice; signing your name; putting on a pair of new socks; reading a sweet poem; petting your cat; throwing a Frisbee for your dog; talking to a friend on the phone; watching a movie; taking a nap on a cold winter afternoon by the fire in your fireplace.

Surely by now you get the drift. Everything and every moment is so endowed with life, mystery and wonder you cannot help but feel so alive you are ready to explode with the vitality of the entire Universe. These things exist in a constant state—how you experience them is your choice. Wake up and live!

9.

Why Do Many People Have Delusions About Themselves And The World?

It takes an unrelenting commitment of objective inquiry to know oneself.

This is a serious problem indeed. Many people perceive things in such a way they distort the truth by twisting it according to their own needs and desires. People do this because they refuse to think clearly. They refuse to question their own motives and they refuse to remove their own preconceptions when studying a subject. In many ways this form of thinking is the essence of all the world's problems. It is the very thing that divides people and tears asunder the sanctity of life. People and nations go to war over the subjective distortions they believe are absolutely correct.

People have delusions about themselves. It takes a rare person to truly understand himself accurately. We all want to think we know who we are and why we do the things we do. But this understanding takes an astute objectivity. It takes a deep and passionate grasp of your inner makeup to sort out the delusions from the truths. Basically, most people do not want to know the truth. They mask their thinking with distortions, which empowers them into feeling a certain way without knowing the history of how they came to these conclusions.

Take the example of ubiquitous political division. People living in the same country are often at odds with each other because of extreme political dissimilarities. For instance, one person thinks the government should be responsible for the education of its children, while another person thinks the government should not have anything to do with the education of its children. They oppose each other strongly. Some people are dedicated to conservative policies, while others are vehemently opposed to them. Where is the objective truth in these cases? What is driving these people to extremely different viewpoints?

Delusions about and distortions of external conditions are behind the thinking of many people. Stubbornness and inflexibility keep people in a tightly sealed chamber without windows to behold a greater range of truths. You must summon the courage to look beyond your own scope to grasp more understanding of your position. There is nothing wrong with having strong positions about subjects. But you need to make sure you are choosing wisely and intelligently, and that your choices serve both you and the world. Strive to see things objectively. Strive to be honest and clear. Strive to study your own motives to sort out the ones constricting your ability to think well.

Delusions are a form of self-obsession and self-control. The more a person becomes rigid in his thinking, the more likely he is going to support his position with a slew of distorted information to buttress this perspective. We all go looking for other people who support our views. We gravitate toward places matching our way of thinking. One of the best ways to gain mastery over this subject is to become more objective. Try to be open by getting exposure to various viewpoints. Collect as much information as possible, sift through it, and then make a choice based upon a sound, rational conclusion.

The more a person can use his mind as an investigative tool, the more he can study both himself and the outside world by reducing the tendency to fall prey to delusions. Decide to be a champion of truth, using a clear lens through which to see the outside world with freshness and openness.

10.

How Can We Have A Healthy Relationship With Money?

You can befriend money by replacing your toxic attachment to it with a healthy attitude.

Money is merely special paper printed with ink. By itself, it has almost no value except the value society places upon it. Money is the bane of many people's lives. It engulfs them; constricts them; tantalizes them and haunts them in such ways some of us lie, cheat, steal and hurt others to obtain it. We place such significance on money we lionize those who have accumulated tons of it and, simultaneously, vilify those who are destitute. Undoubtedly, humans have an enormous, prevalent, attitudinal disease around money.

By itself, money is nothing. It neither has greatness nor misery; it is neither noble nor ignoble; it is not power nor weakness. Money is an exchange system most of the world's societies have adopted. Money is energy because of the worth we collectively place upon it. It is energy used to purchase items such as land, homes, food, clothing, vacations, art, stocks, bonds, insurance, automobiles, boats, medicines, companionship, etc. It is the operating tool we use to survive and to make our lives more comfortable. Without money, living in society becomes an abominable challenge. Destitution is a terrible burden for a person lumbering through the world.

Many people have illusions about money and are caught in an emotional whirlwind over which they feel they have no control. This is a baleful disorder demanding to be healed. The experience of life cannot be comfortable or upbeat without a healthy relationship with money.

The first step in creating a healthy relationship is to understand it for what it is. It is not happiness; it is a means of fulfilling material needs. It is not freedom; it is a way to create more latitude in your life. It is not power; it is a way to amp your love of life to give you more opportunities. It is not spirituality; it is a way to demonstrate your compassion by being generous to others. When you are darting around the money world, chasing it in a huge vacuum like the machines in Las Vegas with bills floating around a plastic cage while you have a few minutes to grab as many of the bills as you can, you become lost in a frenzy of overindulging—without even knowing you are doing it.

When you hoard money, you become the architect of your own incarceration. When you renounce money, you become a victim of it. Those who condemn it are not facing their own issues about money. You must remember money is an energy you can abuse or value and place in its proper perspective. When you use it to create a sense of power, you become a tyrant and a slave to your own denial of fears around money. When you are parsimonious, you choke your life force and end up stifling the resilience that enables you to feel safe and happy in the world.

Bottom line, money needs a major transformation for most people. The answer is balance. Maintain a conscious relationship with money and you will be the creator of your own destiny. Treat money respectfully and you will have harmony with it. Be prudent but not overly thrifty. When you are reckless, spending the money you have without thinking of the consequences, you will get swallowed in debt. Plan for the future, but don't be too overzealous because your experience of the now will suffer. There were people who lived an unpleasant, deprived life whose relatives found a cache of a million dollars under their beds after their deaths. The converse is also true: There are those who spend all the money they have and when winter comes they have no shoes to walk in the snow. It is all a matter of balance and harmony.

Your relationship to money is a reflection of how you trust the world and how you trust yourself. If you are relaxed around the subject of money you will feel safe and protected. If you are uptight, secretive, fearful around the subject of money, you will shrink and shrivel at the slightest hint of something pulling at your money hang-ups. Don't let the idea of money sabotage your love of life. Don't let it ruin your day, week, month and years. We all have a finite amount of time on this planet. How we handle money will, in many ways, dictate how meaningful our journey becomes.

Many people also don't allow themselves the luxury of earning good money for the services they render. When you feel good about money, it will flow more easily to you. Earning money is your right. If you have reservations or guilt about how much you receive, then you need to examine why you want to sell yourself short. There are covert hostilities lurking inside the psychology of how you feel about yourself. Accumulating money becomes a passport to a vast array of opportunities. Circulate your money; keep it humming as you traverse your way through life. Keep money flowing to you and from you—and you will be on top of it. You will then be the beneficiary of money.

Spiritual people often try to discard the idea of money from their lives. This is a fallacy. Money and spirituality are intertwined. These people cannot avoid money no matter how determined they are to discount its significance. At the same time, keep the subject of money in a healthy place in the greater scheme of things. Often people with a lot of money are perceived as being more successful than others. This is not true. If you have been fortunate to acquire significant money, you should be grateful and humble.

Pure spirituality is about balance in the world. Live with love; give to others; take care of yourself; treat money reverentially as you would treat a garden you have personally cultivated. This becomes the bridge to a wonderful life where you taste the ripest fruits in the garden of plenty and share with others what you have grown in your quest of divinity and of life's most precious experiences! Use money in a constructive and conscious way, trusting what it can do to enhance your life—and then feel yourself celebrating existence with passion and joy!

11.

How Can We Instill In Ourselves A Sense Of Humor?

Laughter lights up our souls and connects us to the purity of our inner child!

Walk to the metaphorical edge of the known territory you have explored your entire life. When you are ready to leap into the unknown by leaving everything behind you, with a sense of boundless joy, raise your arms, turn around and then start strutting like an exuberant chicken as you make your way back into the world. Put simply: Don't take yourself too seriously. Look for things to laugh about and to make others laugh. Humor is an antidote for the woes of your life. Play with the world; see the humor in everything; laugh with it. Bring your laughter and hilarity to others. It is contagious. Laughter will release your toxins, making you feel alive and happy.

It doesn't matter if someone is generally more comic and wittier than you or was born with a talent for making others laugh. Humor is about letting go of rigidity. It is about diving into the absurd with all the gusto in your soul. It is about taking a part of you and putting on a comical mask that leaves you in uproarious laughter. You will feel free and aligned with your deepest self. Laugh, play, celebrate and rejoice. Then you can teach others about the gift of living in the moment.

12.

How Can People Better Connect With Others?

When we touch another's life, we open the portals leading us to new places of joy and fulfillment within ourselves!

This question is in many ways the root of all human struggles. The lack of meaningful connection with other people causes emotional issues with serious consequences. Without sustainable, special connections with other people, the human soul withers and becomes brittle. This is a chronic, slow, debilitating disorder experienced by a huge number of people to some extent.

People need the company of others. They need the energy of intimacy and camaraderie in friendship in order to help balance themselves. They need connections with others to feel at peace with life. Without integrating friendships, a person will feel a void in his or her life. A terrible emptiness will linger inside until it is healed. We are social beings who are not meant to be alone for a long period of time. The repercussions of protracted aloneness are many, including aberrant views, behavior and temperament.

What causes the schism between people is multifaceted and complex. One of the most salient aspects is self-centeredness. When a person is immersed in his own affairs, there is little space for another person. When a person is obsessed with his own life, he will shut out others, forcing them to stay away. The self-centered person wants to connect with other people and form meaningful relationships, but is so caught up in himself he is sabotaging the process of getting his basic needs met. People do not want to be close to someone preoccupied with himself. This form of immaturity will also adversely interfere with the person's reasoning systems and creativity. Extreme egoism is a one-way road to a living nightmare.

Another reason people are not able to connect well with others is fear. Fear of rejection is so powerful many people hide behind a cautious veneer that keeps the interaction with others on a fleeting, superficial level. Vulnerability is terrifying for many people. Being at the mercy of another person who could hurt and disappoint is so insidious it can keep a person trapped in a protective identity for life.

It takes boldness and courage to reach out to another person. It is risky to walk the emotional gauntlet of another person, having to pass various tests, before reaching his or her heart. The dynamics of human friendship are often fraught with complex agendas not easily identifiable.

But the rewards of friendship are worth all the risks in the world. We all know how uplifting it is to be in the company of someone who knows us well. There is a remarkable depth of love in special friendships. This love often makes the difference between living a life of mediocrity or a life of wonderful fulfillment.

One of the ways you can meet a person for the first time is to take an enthusiastic interest in him.

When you meet a person, you are discovering an entirely new planet whose landscape and atmosphere are unknown to you. Each person alive today is a separate, fascinating and unexplored new world. Take a great interest in a new person. Never assume you know him; never try to limit him by classifying the person in your mind. Be thrilled to discover this new person with his own spectacular history, evolution and weather patterns. Be excited to enter this new environment with an open, appreciative and inquisitive attitude. When you take a genuine interest in another person he will usually be delighted to show you the treasures of who he is.

Another facet of connecting with others is to give of yourself. Give of your wisdom; your laughter; your passion; your creativity; your love of beauty; your time; your listening from the heart; your compassion; your song that makes you unique among all the people on Earth. And when two people connect well and form a lasting friendship, there is no other event in life that can surpass this experience.

13.

How Can I Cultivate More Self-Esteem And Confidence?

The more we cultivate deep self-esteem, the more effective we are with every endeavor we embark upon.

L iving a joyous, fulfilling life is directly related to the level of self-esteem you have about yourself. The formula for engaging successfully with other people requires an inner confidence, allowing you to express yourself freely and aiding you to be receptive to others. We are all social beings, eager to connect in meaningful ways with other people.

Without a strong sense of inner confidence, the world becomes a hostile, threatening place. To avoid feeling hurt by the negligence of others, we implode and retreat from the world, finding safety in our hermetically sealed illusion of protection. Although this condition separates us from others and reduces the chances of getting hurt, it also encroaches on the natural inclination to be close with other people. We need to bond with others; we need intimacy; we need love.

From our earliest childhood, we can recall numerous incidents of rejection, disapproval, chiding, criticism, and even abuse. These unfortunate experiences tore asunder the delicate fibers of our confidence. We were devastated by little barbs that felt catastrophic as people deliberately or unwittingly assailed us in some way. It was, and is, a monumental task to overcome such insidious damage to our self-esteem.

There is a solution to this pervasive dynamic afflicting almost everyone alive. Self-esteem is a solitary journey requiring you to purge the cobwebs of your own psychological makeup. You must do some major spring-cleaning. The people who perpetrated negative things upon you did not have dominion over your worth. You are the only one who can command sovereignty over your life. You are the only one deciding who you are and how valuable you are to yourself. When you let the actions of others dictate your destiny, you are acting as a victim and diminishing your self-esteem at the hands of people and situations that truly have no power over you.

Yes, the hurts you felt in your past were real. But they are over. They serve no purpose in the now. They were not meant to etch dark stains on the exquisite, unsullied beauty of your soul. The cruelty of others is their lesson to unravel. They are also trapped in some form of pain.

It is your responsibility to develop your own self-esteem. You alone can build bridges to your highest self to find the masterpiece intrinsically living within you. You are not the incidents of hurts you have endured over your lifetime.

You are an unduplicated genius of the spiritual world that has given you the gift of experiencing yourself in material form. Cherish yourself. Own your power to love yourself—not through the trappings of your ego—but through the light of your love affair with life. When you discover the miracle of which you are made, your sense of confidence and self-esteem will ignite in spectacular fireworks that can only be seen with your eyes. When you forgive those who have hurt you and have healed your own wounds, the only path you can possibly follow is the one of immense confidence as you dance jubilantly all the way through the rest of your life!

14.

Why Can't People Make The Changes That Will Help Them?

The challenge of making constructive changes in our lives is proportional to the sense of peace we can achieve.

People are attached to their patterns. They feel comfortable in them and don't want to relinquish them, regardless of how counterproductive these patterns are and how self-denigrating they make the person feel. If someone truly wants to change a habit it will be done. The operative words here are: wants to change. Most people, despite showing strong desires, do not want to change. They say they do and demonstrate to others and even to themselves they want to change—but deep inside they cling tenaciously to the old patterns.

When a person wants to change something, it is done relatively quickly and effortlessly. If someone sees a speeding train racing down the tracks he is crossing, he jumps as fast as he can without thinking. This doesn't require much analysis. Jump or die. Making the decision was easy. Taking the action was easy. The person wanted to live. He was not on a suicide mission. Although it is true that most bad habits or traits don't require a split-second decision over life or death, most people are not ready to jettison these habits for a better life for themselves. If they were ready, the change would happen. In order to change a lifetime pattern, a person must work assiduously for days and months to reinforce the new pattern.

15.

How Can People Learn To Be Satisfied With What They Have?

When we can find satisfaction with our destiny, we have entered the realm of what is considered enlightenment.

Being satisfied does not mean you disown the passion for improvement. Aspiring to reach higher places in your life is a good thing. Striving for goals is also a healthy thing to do. Expanding, growing and finding greater joy in life is the beat to which most of us march. The higher you aim, the better. But if your happiness depends on achieving the dreams you have set for yourself, then you will be caught in the winds of dissatisfaction. When this happens the world dims, casting a pall over you as you continue on your destiny. You become trumped by the very dreams you have created.

The art of living well has one basic component that supersedes everything else. It is simply living in the moment—delighted, satisfied, uplifted. It is finding a deep appreciation, an inner peace with what is happening all around you. It is not complacency or resignation. It is loving the existence you are experiencing with such a sense of pleasure and appreciation that nothing can steal the moment from you.

The mind functions as a ceaseless machine wanting more, living in the past and toying with ideas about the future. This is not healthy and will only lead to dissatisfaction. One of the main purposes of the mind is to fix things that are broken or incomplete.

Satisfaction is the antithesis of what keeps the mind running. When you feel good about the external circumstances of any given moment, the mind's operating system is not required.

The key to being satisfied is to enjoy the unfolding process in every second as you pursue your dreams. Contentment is a beautiful feeling. It is a bridge buttressed with love that allows you to cross any chasm with a sense of safety, knowing you will reach the other side.

When you feel satisfied in the moment, the world slows down for you so you begin to see its wonders. When you reach this state, you can tap into the reservoir of talents that makes you a genius. We are all geniuses once we cross the bridge to the paradise of loving life in the now!

16.

Why Don't People Listen Well And What Can I Do To Become A Better Listener?

There are many ways to listen to the world, and each one brings us closer to understanding the mystery of life.

Listening is one of the most potent forms of understanding and of connecting with life. It is about opening your mind fully and ardently to something outside of yourself. Most people are swirling around their own inner magnetic trance; they are engulfed in themselves. To listen requires that you leave behind your inner dialogue, entering a new frontier without the trainloads of your own personal opinions and biases. This is an art form where you need to become an anthropologist discovering an exotic lost tribe in the jungle. Everything you hear and witness goes directly into your being without the filters of your own predilections and predispositions! Listening is total freedom, focusing on the now.

Every person has a vast history with endless stories, feelings, ideas and opinions. Listening with your heart and with the complete concentration of your being means that you are willing to suspend all the values you own and come into this person's world eager to discover, to learn, to understand with a new set of tools. These tools are invented as the story unfolds. They are energies of synergy, compassion, patience and trust. You must trust the person sharing so much that you put your own issues on hold.

People find learning about someone else so difficult because they are too buried in their own stories. Your story has nothing to do with another person. It is only when you are willing to drop your story and enthusiastically enter into another person's world, can you begin to be a good listener. The more you develop an astute sensitivity to the subtleties around you, the more you will find tiny jewels that shine in the dark, eventually leading you to a treasure trove. There is not a person alive whose unduplicated life is not teeming with wonders. It is a terrible tragedy that few of us are willing to listen to these wonders.

It takes time to listen to another. It takes enormous empathy. It takes calmness and gentleness to hear the nuances of the other person. Most of us are too quick to interject, to offer our ideas or to find the dents in their logic or to point out we don't understand. Oftentimes we fall into a passive state of boredom where we feign interest, but in truth we are falling asleep.

The deeper we attune ourselves to another person's story, the more the gulf between souls shrinks and we land in a special place inspiring us because we have experienced a rare moment of truly understanding and of being understood.

17.

Why Do Many People Seem To Live In The Past?

The past controls our lives only to the degree we refuse to free ourselves from it.

People live in the past because they haven't resolved its issues or they are not comfortable with living in the present. The past can often seem like a fairyland to a person dissatisfied with his life. The past also represents a time of playfulness and innocence, and it is hard for a person to let it go, to jettison it into the unknown because it forms the basis of how he perceives his authentic self.

It's true: the past can harbor many sweet and nostalgic memories. And these memories should be held in a sacred place in your history. You can revisit the past, but you cannot relive it. Keep the past in its proper place in the grand scale of who you are right now.

The biggest problem with people who frequently allude to their past is this form of thinking limits them from being fully present in the now. It also keeps them a prisoner to the issues still lingering within them, which cripple them on an emotional and energetic level. There are people who were told by a parent over and over they should not speak because they have nothing to say. Then, when they are at old age, they still have a hard time expressing themselves because they believe they have nothing to say. They keep playing the same inner dialogue over until it becomes an intrinsic pattern to their psychological makeup.

The past is over! It no longer holds dominion over you. It was a reality yesterday, but today you can reinvent who you want to be. You cannot remove the past or alter it. But what you can do is to place your attention on the now and choose the path you wish to follow. It doesn't take much to become the master of your destiny. It takes only courage to take charge of your life. If you keep failing by returning to the past, you are not willing to give it up. You are not willing to heal yourself. You may think you are and you may think you are making progress. But until you can successfully move forward, you have one foot stuck in your past.

There are people who spend hundreds of hours in therapy to unravel the past. They spend years and decades to unhinge the power of the past from them. They use drugs and hypnosis and other means to launch themselves into freedom from the past. Most of the time this does not work because the only way to free yourself from the tangles of the past is to stand at the helm of your ship and set sail by your own devices toward the sunrise of a new day. In other words, you alone must master the pull and burden of living in the past. You alone must master this confinement by taking charge of your life. You must find the resources to achieve this at all costs. Ultimately, after all the help from outside sources, you alone are responsible for reclaiming your destiny and your life!

18.

How Can I Become A
Positive Person?

*When we remember the countless great
things in life that far outnumber the bad
things, we are building the mental pathways
to positivity.*

It is not one extreme or the other with the mind. It is
not about being all positive or all negative. There are
many dichotomies and mysterious dynamics in the
world. The key to being fully alive and at peace is to be able
to control the many thoughts rushing through the mind
by not shunning them or suppressing them. The key is to
master what you think by being in charge of your mind.

Never let your mind run amok with thoughts. Never let
your own emotions take over how you see the world. When
you have unresolved fears and hurts deeply lodged in

74

your body, they will come racing to the surface when you are confronted by things reminding you of the pain still buried within you. Then your thoughts will be influenced by this pain and your perceptions will be distorted. You will start seeing the world through a semi-opaque lens fused with the emotions of fear living inside you.

You are in charge of your thoughts. Find out why you feel a certain way about a person. Where do these feelings come from and how were they formed? Probe yourself for the answers. Be willing to delve into the labyrinths of your soul to find the answers. But don't try to deny your thoughts or insist you think positively about things. This is a form of self-manipulation and will only keep you prisoner to the blinders you have forgotten you have donned.

Thoughts and beliefs are the most powerful entities controlling human behavior. They are the precursors to action. Beliefs and values are learned mostly by unconscious events and programs indoctrinated over our lifetimes. Be conscious of where your beliefs originated; be aware of who is in charge of these beliefs and if they are valid and serve a purpose.

The more conscious you become the more enthralled and delighted with life you will be. You will not be threatened by negative thoughts because these will always be overshadowed by the light of who you are.

Remember, when you direct your attitudes and mind to be positive, you are setting the stage for a more vibrant and enjoyable ride through life. Many people have jaundiced positions about subjects. If you can remove the negative preconceptions, you will find yourself engaged more fully and more enthusiastically in activities. The gift of a generally positive mindset is it gives you a lighter, freer and happier ride through the world.

19.

How Does One Remain Sane
In This World?

*Sanity is a way of life that requires focus,
effort and a healthy consciousness.*

S
anity is not a given state. It must be learned. All of us entered the world with a pretty empty slate, a clean canvas upon which we draw the experiences of our lives. Every society roils with some form of chaos and disorder. There is a pathological pulse driven by fear and insecurity. We land in our parent's unhealed, emotionally ruptured scene; we deal with intense struggles of fitting in at school; we are requested to grow up by the time we are sixteen or eighteen years old. We are expected to do

well in some career; adjust well to our communities; find a good mate, propagate and raise children in a healthy environment; and manage to advance our economic status in the midst of a sea churning with challenging waves that can knock us over in an instant!

Daunting things surround us on a daily basis. It is easy to get swallowed by the rising tides of emotional tribulation. It is easy to fall from the safety of a stable boat while trying to navigate past formidable boulders in our way that can capsize our lives in the blink of an eye.

No wonder many of us suffer some form of insanity. Becoming sane is a journey without end, requiring constant vigilance and dedication.

The journey of sanity requires a strong inner resolve to handle daily tasks of survival with a good attitude: hopeful, resourceful, positive, calm and confident. Being sane means that you have a passionate love affair with life. You feel fulfilled and upbeat most of the time. You like your work and you enjoy earning money, using it to enhance your life by adding a nice assortment of material things to make your life fun and convenient. At the same time, you are not a slave to possessions, making them greater than they are. You also enjoy being generous and know that money is merely a means to an end and it doesn't rule your life.

Sanity means you love who you are and take wonderful care of your body. It also means you love other people—not just a few of them predicated upon how they make you feel and what they do for you. It is about cherishing the lot of humanity in all its wild diversity. Compassion and sanity are intertwined. You love old people and children and everyone in between. You go out of your way to be kind to strangers; you let drivers go ahead of you in a long line of cars. You also love animals and treat them with reverence and compassion.

You like your own company and experience restoration in solitary walks in the countryside. You have your own spiritual relationship and allow for the expression of the deity of others by respecting their choices. You are always growing and open to new ideas. Every day you add a new piece of information of truth to your vast accumulation of data you've collected over your lifetime. You never flaunt what you know; you share your understanding gently when others are receptive.

Being sane is cultivating kindness, joy and laughter. It is about treating each day as if it were the first of your life—full of adventure, surprises and excitement. You celebrate the gift of life with a flare that is your own special signature.

This world, often convulsing from a chronic disease of suffering and struggle, needs you and you give freely of yourself to make the world a better place for all creatures. Sanity has enabled you to release the talons of emotional predation from your mind and heart so that you can love life and all its variety. Sanity is its own reward.

20.

What Is The Best Way To Protect Oneself Against Mishaps?

With all the fears besetting our lives, the best thing we can do to protect ourselves is to develop a positive and nurturing attitude.

Stop thinking about them. Around us are innumerable possibilities that may harm us or even kill us. The human mind is wired to be extremely vigilant, watching for cracks in the road so we don't stumble and break our leg. The idea of a surprise attack is scary; at any given moment an uninvited catastrophe may strike us. Can we do anything about this? No. In truth we don't control the world and we certainly don't control the actions of most others.

But what we can do is stop giving energy and attention to this subject. By giving energy to a possible harm we send out the vibrations that go looking for the very thing we dread. When we surround ourselves with a feeling of safety, we are enhancing our chances of being protected. What we think sets the stage for the drama to unfold. Worry and consternation about being a victim of a disease or a shooting or a mugging or destitution will only foster the right ingredients, making us a prime target for these abhorrent things to happen.

Spirit is the ultimate protection. But spirit is not some outside entity, some little invisible creature hovering over you, fending off disease, attack, misfortune with a wave of its wand. Spirit is the energy you engender through the feelings you own about the way you experience life. Spirit is the thoughts you keep to yourself as you walk down the street or when you can't sleep at night. Spirit is what passes through your body, entering the deepest cavern of your soul, when you move through the daily activities of your life.

The more joyous you are, the more your spirit is in rhythm with the world. The more trusting you are, the higher you leap along the path with a jaunty disposition. The more loving you are, the safer the world becomes for you. These are the things that will keep you buoyed, relaxed, safe, energized, eager, happy and triumphant as you move through the physical world.

The power of a vivacious, robust and exhilarated way of seeing life cannot be measured. These are the things that can't be taken away from you. These are the things that propel you forward in your thirst to drink from the fountain of life's ecstasy!

21.

Why Do Some People Become Bullies, Racists And Terrorists And How We Can Heal Them?

The abrasive acts of a person can be changed through the right guidance and love.

The heinous things individuals perpetrate on others leave wounds lasting for a lifetime. This question is one of the most important ones we, as conscious beings, can ask ourselves. It is a vital question because, if we can find answers, everyone will benefit from a deeper discovery and understanding. None of us can step outside the virulent, contemptuous actions of people deliberately harming, maiming and killing others for no reason except for the irreconcilable hatred festering in their minds. This is one of the lowest points in the chronicles of human evolution.

Most bullies are young people, but older people can also act as bullies. A bully is a weak person trying to wield power over another for the sake of deriving a vicarious sense of control. A bully is a coward who is afraid of being weak. He therefore seeks out others who are not socially or physically strong, and unleashes his sadistic cruelty. There is, in his psyche, a warped pleasure at seeing someone else suffer because the bully is accomplishing two major things by acting out. One, he is releasing his own pent up hostility and hurts onto an easy target. Two, he is deflecting his own pain by placing it on his victim.

This aberrant form of behavior was learned from a series of abuses and hurts a bully endured in the first years of his life. He felt helpless, unable to defend himself from the blows of the person who was more powerful. This vulnerability and helplessness infuriated the bully, causing him to grow suspicious of people. The suspicion led to a deep disdain for others, especially weak peers who were unable to defend themselves.

Healing a bully will require a massive therapeutic process. He will have to uncover all the unconscious layers of his own pain and release them through forgiveness and compassion. He will also have to learn how to love himself and others without fear, intimidation and suspicion. In time he will need to learn to trust others, allowing himself to feel vulnerable and yet remain safe.

Much of the bullying in schools can be reduced if all the teachers, parents, and administrators become aligned in a unified campaign to end bullying. They would need to agree to a zero tolerance for bullying; a potent program to rehabilitate the bully; communicate and teach compassion and empathy; create an environment where everyone is treated with respect and kindness. Bullying is a prevalent disorder that can be unlearned if the people in charge make it a top priority by utilizing every resource available to them.

Racism is one of the most despicable forms of ignorance in the world. A racist, like the bully, is a person riddled with fear who has taken this fear and placed it upon an entire group of people, blaming them for his own woes or the troubles of the whole world. The racist is also a coward because he or she refuses to look at his own insecurities, taking responsibility for the plight of his life. It is easier to blame a group of people than to find the cause within himself.

Racism is also fueled by a group mindset. All the poisonous tributaries of each individual come together in a ferocious confluence of energy, flooding the group mentally with hatred, which is very difficult to stop. When a person is swept into the group energy it becomes almost impossible to maintain the integrity of his own thinking. This is why entire societies can support vile actions against millions of innocent people. A racist is an adult bully.

Curing the racist is easy. Have him go live with the group of people against whom he is racist. Have him learn the customs, mannerisms and lifestyles of these people and he will surely find not only their humanity but also his own.

When I was young, I was taught to treat a guest who came to visit us with more kindness and respect than I showed my own family. A neighbor or person from another culture or of a different race or nationality was a special visitor to our home. We became the ambassadors of our race and everything we did was a reflection of our people, our family. Giving love to strangers, making them feel welcomed in our home was the powerful tenet by which we lived. This, of course, was taught to me. Teach a racist how to love those who are different; teach him how to empathize with and appreciate another culture or race of people—and he will find elements of the beauty within himself that have been long buried underneath the walls of his own fear.

The terrorist is a combination of a bully and a racist whose mind has been infiltrated with acrimonious hatred. He is a person who has lost his own individuality, swept into the fervor of some maniacally intolerant movement that demands its way or death. The terrorist's mind has been taken over by fear of the outside to such an extent that his own life has no purpose except to destroy the enemy. This type of mind is lost in the values of the group that cannot differentiate between right and wrong, good and evil. He perceives anyone belonging to the other group as the incarnation of evil itself and must be destroyed. No one is exempt from the terrorist's mentality of war against the world—not children, people who have never heard of his cause, animals and elders who might even have sympathy for his struggles. The vision of the terrorist is so narrow he can't even see the difference between day and night. He lives in continuous darkness, seething like a volcano ready to erupt.

Despite the severity of the terrorist, he or she is still a human being. Although his mind has been taken over by some fanatical organization, he still can be saved. It will take a herculean effort on the part of his friends and family, if they can reach him. Show him love; show him how violence and hatred only intensify the suffering of the world; show him that he can belong to civilization when his heart opens and his mind becomes clear. If we can save one terrorist from falling into a funnel of death and destruction, we have made the world a little safer and a little more peaceful.

22.

Is Our Life A Toss Of The Dice Or Is There Something Behind Our Destinies?

No one truly knows the mystery behind our lives, but rest assured that whatever keeps us floating through the world does so naturally.

I n our fervent attempts to understand this world, we try hard to find reasons behind our lives. We strive to understand and then elucidate this to ourselves and to others. In actuality, as much as we don't want to believe it, we cannot know the complete truth behind our lives. We cannot even begin to find the vast world of causation—let alone attempt to explore it.

It is best to accept this limitation with a gracious attitude. It is also best to subdue the arrogance our egos place over us and then surrender by flowing with life. In our attempts to understand, we place enormous weight on our rather narrow points of view. We like to think we are masters of the world; in reality we are mere servants to forces we cannot begin to fathom—let alone control.

The conditions of our lives, such as our parents and where we were born, mean little next to the supreme gift spread before us—the opportunity for irreversible emancipation! This is what matters and is endowed with power: What we do with our lives in the now, how we choose the path before us and how we decide to move through it and what we do with the things we find along the way? These are the questions we need to ask. These are the things we must find within ourselves that will propel us forward in our unpredictable, short, mystical journey through this life. These are the questions that should float through our brains and will undoubtedly shoot us into a new orbit around the blazing light of existence!

23.

Why Are Some Marriages Fraught With Problems That End In Divorce?

Sustaining a marriage is done primarily through clear and compassionate communication.

Marriage is the ultimate commitment two people make to each other to become partners in life as a result of their deep affection, adoration and love for each other. They have come to this sacrosanct place because they found much fulfillment, joy and compatibility together. It is one of the most important milestones in a person's life. Marriage is a unified partnership to share dreams, hopes, bodies, money, home and souls together. This is a grand adventure for two lovers.

However, the actual joining of two separate people on a lifetime journey engenders a slew of challenges and issues. It is a monumental task to entwine yourself with another person on both surface and deep levels. All of the nuances of the other person's personality come flaring on to the scene. Adjusting to each other requires tremendous patience and compromise. Herein lies the problem: How do two distinctly different people learn to harmonize together when all of the furtive, unresolved issues explode at the wrong moments, forcing them to confront the shadows of their partner and of themselves? How do they manage to overcome the emotional upheavals that sweep over them like an avalanche? How do they negotiate with each other when there is sharp pain and fear sweeping through them?

No one can escape the inevitable issues a marriage will produce. These issues, when not resolved, will actually grow more intense the longer the couple stays together. The reason many marriages are fraught with problems and end in divorce is the limited capacity to get beyond conflicts. Without a massive healing, the conflicts in a marriage will grow more sinister in time until they become intolerable. This is why many couples go to marriage counselors but still end up getting a divorce.

There is a solution to helping a marriage survive and even thrive. Each person must summon the strength to go beyond his personal issues and serve the other with immense patience, kindness and compassion. He must own his issues and take responsibility for them. This is a most challenging thing to achieve. He must also be unwavering in his commitment to remain with his partner throughout the long battles. Both of the partners must stay true to their promise of keeping the marriage alive to the end of life.

Too many men and women depart from a problematic marriage prematurely. Sometimes it takes years to mend things; derailment occurs less frequently as time passes. The marriage always needs fresh ideas to nurture it. It needs much care and sensitivity. It must be treated with the greatest reverence the way you would treat your own newborn child. You wouldn't ignore her; you wouldn't neglect her. You would be extremely aware of her needs and would do everything in your capacity to keep her happy and healthy. This same attitude is needed for both members of the marriage.

Marriage must also be an inviolable institution held closest to your heart. You must have mutually agreed upon principles that cannot be broken. You must share your deepest thoughts with your beloved and work out any differences that might wedge between the two of you.

If things become disfigured and incapable of repairing, then you must separate and call it quits. This is the last option to pursue because it is so final.

Marriage can work well. But it will force you to stretch your boundaries way beyond anything you have ever known. If you can do this with gladness, caring and love, there will be no limits to the depth of love you can reach.

24.

What Can We Do To Get Out Of Ourselves And Help Someone Else?

There is no more rewarding act than to aid others in making their lives better.

Go out and take action. It is that simple. Organize your week by deciding how much time you want to volunteer for some charitable cause. Discipline yourself by making it happen. Don't think about it, don't procrastinate, and don't make excuses why you can't do it. Do it! You are not in the way. You are the way. When you think you are in the way, you are using this as an excuse to avoid helping others because you truly don't want to do it. A part of you thinks it should offer to help others; another part of you has not made it a priority.

Many people bounce all over the inner map of their emotions, scrambling around in a frenzy of indecision and inaction. This is a disorder called: "I don't want to be responsible for my life so I will play the role of a space cadet!" There's nothing complicated about this phenomenon. The essence of it is self-immersion where the individual is indulging emotions that keep him or her on a one-dimensional trajectory through the self. It is a powerful system keeping the status quo intact.

In order to offer love and joy to others you will need to dismantle the elements of rage and condemnation you secretly harbor about the human race. Many people have debris of animosity floating around their inner atmosphere from leftover explosions of hurt, disillusionment and panic. The floating debris interferes with the clear signal from the heart to the mind that knows only love. It causes disturbances that eventually grow into dark, misanthropic and dangerous meteor showers raining down on the garden of love in the soul.

You can remove this debris by advancing your consciousness. Make peace with the shortcomings of others; accept the impediments and inconsistencies; no one is perfect. Don't let your pride swallow you in its lofty, separate and manipulating cauldron. Indignation and self-righteousness separate you from the rest of humanity. This is a grand illusion. Join the human race. Reach out to others. Try to empathize with someone not as fortunate as you. Put yourself into this person's shoes by trying to experience what he goes through on a daily basis. Open your heart and do whatever you can to comfort your fellow humans. By doing so, you bring immeasurable satisfaction to your own life.

25.

What Can Be Done To Be Good Parents And Raise Our Children To Become Better People?

One of the greatest tasks before us is in the raising of our children—done correctly!

One of the most important things we can do to produce a healthy society for future generations is to perfect the raising of our children. Most people don't realize this is a vital issue to saving civilization. We place enormous energy on a plethora of other issues, merely taking for granted the subject of child rearing. Many parents do not have the necessary skills, tools and acumen to raise their children well. It takes a super human effort to bring a child into this world and then to raise him or her supremely well.

There are many criteria that will enable parents to be outstanding role models for their children. It's amazing how innocent a child is when he enters this world. Everything the child experiences on many levels will influence him as he develops into an adult. It is a spectacular journey from day one until a child becomes an adult. What parents do and how they handle their children will become the template for the child's life.

I will expound on some of the more important criteria. One of them is consistency. It's true most of us have a wide range of feelings and behaviors we express in the course of a day or a week. To a child who is completely dependent on his parents, consistency on the part of the parents will quickly build a strong foundation upon which the child can form his own personality, faith, values, and way of beholding the world. Parents need to be consistent, stable, solid, and clear. Yes, we all falter at times. This is only human; but parents who are essentially consistent will aid in helping their children establish a deep security about themselves and a trusting relationship with the world.

The greatest force is love. This sounds self-evident and obvious. It is far from being so. Everyone knows love is all-powerful, enveloping the recipient in a warm, nurturing cocoon. It is rarely manifested in unconditional ways. Love your child deeply and fully without a lot of expectations or conditions. Praise and acknowledge your child as often as you can. Support him by telling him he is capable of anything and assure him how much you admire and care about him no matter what the outcome of some event or activity.

Children become horribly discouraged by the lack of praise and love. Indifference from their parents hurts a child. Some people might construe this as doting on their children. It is not meant to spoil them. It is meant to strengthen them and to help them to build a solid platform from which to operate. The parents don't need to do the work for their child, nor should they be overly protective. They should only offer a pure, unbroken love from their hearts that says to the child: "I will always be there for you and love you immeasurably!"

Another criterion is supporting their imagination and dreams. When you challenge your child to use her imagination without pressuring her, you are giving your child one of the greatest gifts a human can offer. Whatever path your child takes, she is learning about herself and about her world. The human mind possesses unlimited potential. You can serve your child by nudging her into creative arenas and standing on the sidelines to show her you are there in case she needs you.

The next criterion necessary for raising a child to be a healthy adult is setting boundaries and then living impeccably by these boundaries yourself. Most parents fail miserably in this department. A parent can be a paragon of strength by living by the standards he or she has set for himself. Don't contradict yourself. When you do this, you are telling your children boundaries don't matter. Be respectful of the boundaries of others and of your children. This will set an excellent example of trust and reliability.

The last criterion is communication. We all hear the good things about flowing, open, and compassionate communication as a powerful technique in building bridges between people. The biggest mistake parents make is failing to establish a safe, constructive space in which to share thoughts and feelings with their children. Listen to your children. Try to understand them; feel the feelings they have revealed. Never repudiate them and never dismiss your children's feelings. Work together to shine light on the subject to bring insight and resolution. But don't try to fix the problem too quickly. Never be condescending toward your child. Be a pillar of strength and wisdom, but also be willing to learn and to be vulnerable yourself in front of your children. When you communicate together with everyone feeling received, honored and respected, tremendous results happen.

SECTION TWO

Hotly Debated Issues

In this section we get to examine subjects that are highly charged for most people. Here we pause to contemplate these subjects to determine how they impact our personal lives. Through understanding, we can broaden our perspectives by cultivating more empathy for things that might have caused us to react defensively. The questions and answers in this section will give us much to ponder so we can gain greater insight into ourselves and the other people living in the world.

26.

Why Do People Hold On To Hurt and Disappointment for So Long?

It takes tremendous courage and humility to see your part in a conflict.

S ome people cling to misery throughout their lives. What I mean by this is they allow the feeling of the disappointment to seize them, pulling them under into a seething cauldron of pain. When a person feels he has been hurt and disappointed by another, he blames this person as a way to reinforce and justify his anger. A slow, steady fire then burns indefinitely inside his emotions, gradually destroying his love of life.

This fire is fanned by thoughts replaying the same anger winds over and over. Violating someone's pride can turn him into a vindictive person. Many people feel justified in holding a grudge because of the terrible act someone heaped upon them. These people decide to play a victim role, although they don't see it this way. They are displacing all their own inner hurt on to the person whom they deride and condemn.

Why do they keep the fire of discord burning year after year—even when they sometimes can't remember the incident triggering the disconnect from their friend or loved one that happened years earlier? The answer to this complex problem is rooted in the past. In some people there exists a self-destructive tendency that manifests itself in being angry with others as the basis of how they want to experience life. It is not rational, not easy to understand. But in some people the need to harbor resentment, stop communication, and blame someone for years is a hauntingly dark place which somehow gives them ammunition to be quietly furious for the rest of their life. It is a way of reinforcing the idea the world is a harsh, unfriendly, unsafe and hostile place to live. Blaming is a way to prove this to the person.

How do you heal this terrible disorder? How do you get these people to forgive and to reverse the dreaded state they have been locked in for much of their lives?

The person must be willing to sit alone in a room for hours or days to sort through the emotional knots holding him prisoner, untangling every little knot to find out where it came from and why he allowed it to strangle him his entire life. He must be willing to take ownership for his position, forgive himself and then forgive the person against whom he holds his grudge. He must make the overture to the person he has despised by opening his arms with tears in his eyes, saying: "I am sorry! Forgive me! I have made a terrible mistake! I come in peace! I have learned the error of my thinking!"

27.

Why Are Some People Superficial And Only Live On The Surface?

Living with all our senses fully open catapults us into profound experiences.

The human ego is clever, cunning and scheming as it maneuvers through the cracks and byways of your mind. The only obsession this ego has is to protect itself from harm, whether it is real or imagined. Without a clear guidance system to navigate you on your life journey, you will be prone to the controlling manipulation of your ego. You will be doomed to live in a cloistered shell because the ego has prevailed over you. Safety is much easier to manage than to deal with adventure, change, and unexplored frontiers. People find comfort in shallow ponds, swaying in gentle breezes rather than plunging wildly into the turbulent, deeper waves of new experiences.

The same is true for how people talk to others. They stay on the surface of subjects. It is far easier to discuss something outside of a personal realm, like a sporting event last week, than to discuss how you feel about the conflicts you are embroiled in with your supervisor at work. Once people begin to enter superficial spheres, they get accustomed to operating this way. Soon they even begin to think superficially about subjects, including themselves. They go through their long lives dancing to the slow beat of music, never hearing the boom of the drums!

It is a terrible misfortune to wade through the shallow pools of life when there is a plethora of stunning, wonderful experiences just beyond the cemented walls people have built surrounding them. There is the vibrancy and wonder of life everywhere you roam. In every moment the opportunity to learn something new exists. There is excitement and thrill around every bend! There is life sizzling, burnished with the sheen of the heat of a new day! There is the luscious depth of removing the layers of life's mysteries, as if falling into an *Alice In Wonderland* hole when every second something shockingly unexpected lands in the center of your consciousness!

28.

Why Do Many People Resist Social Changes That Will Benefit Almost All Of Us?

We are all in this thing called life together and the more we embrace inclusivity, the more our world gets better for everyone.

People resist social changes because they are fundamentally brainwashed by the pervasive powers that control their lives. The collective attitude of some nations is adverse to social systems that will benefit those who are less fortunate than the super rich. They also have an aversion to social systems because on some visceral level, they fear their freedom and way of life will be threatened.

People love their freedom, and social changes passed by the government are perceived by the limited thinking person as a death sentence that will destroy what is good about his nation. Many people have been assailed by propaganda, telling them their freedom would be severed if they stood by as cowards, allowing socialists to take over their precious values and virtues.

In actuality, nations desperately need a massive overhaul of their infrastructures to bring about social fairness and values. They need a national health plan available to everyone. They need a much healthier work matrix where no one is ever unemployed, where decent conditions and compensation exist. They need educational systems for everyone, not just the rich. They need a revamping of how they treat those who cannot manage well on their own. All of us need a nation where no one is left behind in the pursuit of prosperity and happiness.

The fear of change is entrenched in the national psyche of the people of most countries, preventing them from seeing the truth. This truth is about elevating our thinking to a higher level, enabling every man, woman and child to reap the benefits of a solid, compassionate, inspired and creative nation. Fanatical thinking by people keeps us trapped in darkness. It keeps us stuck in a competitive, harsh, vitriolic, cruel disposition that allows the power-hungry moguls and religious zealots to roll over and enslave those who cannot oppose them.

If you are a person who dreads social changes, you need to take a vision quest for a long weekend to sit in Nature by yourself so you can unravel the beliefs in your head to discover the source from where these beliefs originated. You need to discover the capacity of empathy in your heart. Listen to your higher self. It will shed light upon you, showing you a new path to follow.

29.

Why Do Some People Commit Atrocious Crimes And What Are Your Thoughts About Capital Punishment?

We need to start a humanitarian educational process at the beginning of a person's life with each of us as teachers and healers.

A few of us fall prey to an internal hell in our minds where we cannot think in the same range as a relatively healthy person. This causes depravity in the brain. Coupled with emotional rupturing, the person is disconnected from the mainstream of humanity. He or she feels disempowered and disenfranchised to such an extent that something horrible snaps inside and he is left drowning in a cesspool of insanity boiling with hatred, paranoia, disgust and rage. It doesn't take much to push someone over the edge. These people, who are prime candidates ready to leap into the fire, have in their history countless, accumulated, poisonous wounds that can easily get ignited, setting them on a one-way course into madness.

Nothing is more repugnant and vile to our sensibilities than to hear about the crimes of brutal murder committed by maniacal killers.

What should be done to these people once they are apprehended and proven guilty beyond any doubt? Capital punishment is killing in the name of justice. It is premeditated murder. It is taking a living person and doing something so strong to his body that he will die. This is the ultimate act of torture. Yes, the pain might be fleeting and last only seconds; yes, there may be almost no discernible pain at all.

Nonetheless, a death sentence is about killing the victim. Nothing is more barbaric and sick than to condone, support and allow the death penalty. (At the same time, we should not dismiss or water down the gravity of the crime.) Once we justify the killing of a murderer, we participate in further killing. In some ways the people who carry out the death penalty are falling lower and more maniacally than the criminal himself because these people are rational, sensible, caring, socially-integrated members of society who are just carrying out the orders as stated by their jobs.

Instead of putting an end to the criminal's life, we should take away his freedom and many of his privileges by keeping him in humane, comfortable conditions for the rest of his life. This person has lost his right to live free. Yes, there is no way this exonerates the criminal and in no way is his punishment ever enough to redress the crime committed. But at least there is some accountability and society is protecting itself from this person who might kill again in the future. Rehabilitating this person would be a prodigious undertaking.

In order to advance ourselves as an ever-expanding civilization, we need to examine some of the established institutions that have existed for centuries to see if they uphold the higher morals we want to promulgate for future generations. Take the example of the Coliseum of the ancient Roman Empire. We all know about this form of entertainment where people would sit in their seats watching the victims being savagely killed in a variety of ways for no other purpose but to satisfy the lust for gore by the citizens of that society. Today such entertainment would be unthinkable. At some time in the future, people will look at our accepted norm of the death penalty the way we look aghast at the butchery of ancient Rome.

30.

What Causes A Person To Be Gay/Lesbian And Should Their Marriages Be Legalized?

Love expressed in any way empowers the world.

Most beings are born with their sexual preferences. People can also develop their sexuality through a complicated network of experiences, both conscious and unconscious. All of us are predisposed to a certain preference; others are working out issues that are deep-rooted in their psyches. Every person is a compilation of many forces shaping his or her sexuality.

Each of us has the potential to be bisexual and explore loving a person from either gender. Each of us can, under certain circumstances, lean one way or the other. What is most important is how society accepts gays and bisexuals and how equitably they are treated and respected because their sexual lifestyle is different than the majority. We should cease treating someone as not equal because of his or her sexual lifestyle with the same sex.

A person's sexual choice does not need the inflexibility of our condemnation that only creates separation, mistrust and fear. The rest of us need to be far more tolerant and accepting of other people's sexual lives.

Marriage between two adults is a consecration of their love. Whether it is between two men or two women, society needs to honor and allow for the expression of this love. We can do a great justice to every member of our society by respecting the choices made and to treat everyone decently and kindly. We are all in this life together. When all of our differences are united, we help to create an indomitable force paving the way for a better future.

31.

Why Is There Hunger In The World And How Can It Be Solved?

All of us need to take action to solve this problem.

Hunger is a pathetic, terrible curse for millions of humans. It is one of the most tragic things happening to humanity. Starvation and malnourishment take down many children every year. The cause of this problem is not the lack of the production of food. It is the distribution of the abundant supply of food on the planet that causes the issue. Access to good food is a brutal struggle for many societies, especially for the ones existing in remote locations. These societies do not have the resources or funds to facilitate getting food to their people. There is also rampant corruption within the infrastructures responsible for the distribution of food. The consequence of this defective process is often the slow death of many innocent children and their parents. It is one of the saddest examples of bureaucratic incompetence in the world.

The solution seems relatively easy to implement, but for many reasons it fails to achieve its objective. The developed, wealthy nations have ample surplus food to offer those nations with a starvation problem. Getting the food to these needed places is a major obstacle. The closer the needed food gets to its recipients, the more impediments there are to overcome until most of the food is ruined or lost or gone due to ineptitude of local governments.

All the wealthy nations of the world need to unite in tackling this problem. They need to create a unified system to make sure staple food gets shipped to the destination in time to prevent death from starvation. The United Nations needs to lead this global program as a top priority. There should be systems in place to prevent corruption on local levels. There should be an extensive array of competent directors leading the way for the successful distribution of food to all needy peoples of the world.

Each of us must get behind this cause. We need to take action and to do everything within our capacity to influence a positive outcome. Write letters; join organizations pleading for action; donate monies; and urge our government officials to get involved immediately to help save millions of our fellow humans from the horrors of starvation!

32.

What Are Your Thoughts About Gun Control?

Do we really want to put lethal weapons in the hands of anyone?

I don't believe in gun control because I don't believe in guns. Guns are machines that fire searing-hot missiles at living things for the purpose of killing them. To me, a gun is a small version of a rocket shooting a nuclear missile at a target. They both blast away their victims, obliterating the sacred life force. My position about guns and weapons is they should all be melted down and used in a constructive way for the benefit of everyone. Guns should be abolished.

I know my position doesn't carry much weight and is impractical. I realize this. I also cannot be a conscious being who loves all life by supporting the manufacturing, distribution and use of weapons whose singular purpose is to nullify the sanctity of a living being—whether it is a person, bird, reptile or animal. Killing is wrong. It is unconscionable, horrible. When you love life you cannot harm it. When you have reverence for the miracle of each living thing, you cannot justify killing because of some seething rage or hurt in yourself.

We use guns and weapons to protect ourselves from invasions. We use them to defeat the enemy in wars. We use them to take down others whom we declare to ourselves as unworthy of life. And we use them to keep our societies functioning so madmen don't unleash an avalanche of destruction upon innocent masses.

What a tragic statement this is about our species. In our evolution as systems of groups of people living together, we created guns as a way of warding off danger. Guns are used to battle the demons we have inside ourselves that we project onto others. Guns give us a sense of omnipotence over others. They reduce the playing field to a game of life and death. We flirt with death by brandishing our guns when threatened or out of revenge. We kill our own kind and other species. Even children use guns to kill.

When a bullet ends one life, we have spit in the eye of creation. When one person kills another, all of us are participants in the global insanity of murder. When we condone the use of guns, we are a part of the collective pain of killing that incinerates the beauty of the human soul!

33.

What Is The Best Way To Cope With All The Negative Things Happening In The World?

Few of us realize that we have within us the power to navigate our destinies.

There is no doubt that negative things exist on many levels and some of them, because of their magnitude, are rupturing the sanctity of life. Negativity can pulverize us, hurtling us into an apocalyptic funnel. The events of the day—whether a disaster, an unspeakable crime, an economic collapse, or a tragedy befallen nice people—come to us in shocking waves through apertures of information that slither their way into our minds. This truth cannot be denied.

However, as tragic as these negative events are, there are a thousand times more good things taking place in every second on Earth. Great and wondrous events sustain the planet and keep you and me alive. Take a simple thing like a breath of sweet air without which we'd be dead in a few minutes. How stupendous is this feat of Nature? Yet we hardly seem to notice it or rarely pay homage to it.

Millions of people stopped today to smile at someone. Bursts of laughter came thundering from the mouths of children across the globe. Multitudes volunteered to help others in need. Countless individuals read a great book today or enjoyed watching a flight of geese overhead. Most of us ate a delicious meal and quenched our thirst with refreshing water. We slept soundly in our beds and awoke with a song in our hearts. I could go on indefinitely extolling the virtues happening all the time in this world.

Existence has duality in that there are good things and bad things occurring all the time. We have a tendency to take the good things for granted; the bad things cause a rippling of fear and disgust rolling through us. Negative things haunt us because they threaten us, uprooting the sense of security we all cling to strongly. The negative things we hear about make us feel vulnerable, reminding us of things violating our principles that cry for life, happiness and serenity. We react strongly to the outside world; this is our nature. We ride a turbulent, wild current through a sea of mystery. We cannot change the fundamental nature of this sea. Our destiny is fixed. We live, we learn, we change, we discover, we acquire and let go, we grow old, we die. Welcome to human life.

Coping with negativity is a challenge. It is difficult to minimize the gravity of some of these things. And no one should. At the same time, if you focus on these things, allowing them to engulf you emotionally, you then have lost your freedom and your love of life. This serves no purpose except to harm you as an individual. It takes a heavy toll on you, saddling you with worry, trepidation and hopelessness. The best way to cope with the negative things of the world is to not give them as much credence in your own personal life. Be aware of them and then move on. If you feel compelled to take action, then do something constructive to help resolve the causes of the problem.

Remember to move on and for every second you stumble into a dungeon of negativity, spend ten times more looking around at the things that make life a glorious event! Consciousness is a powerful tool. Direct your own consciousness to serve you and you will then serve the world. Every time you fall into a maelstrom of negativity you contribute to your own demise in small, harmful ways. This does not empower you, make you feel more alive, or help you to help others. It is a form of self-destruction weakening your hold on life. It is in some ways akin to taking poison to make you feel sick. Ask yourself why you do this? Ask yourself if this is serving you or helping to serve others. You don't have to cope with the negatives floating around the world. Just be aware of them and use them to strengthen your capacity to be compassionate, loving, resourceful, useful and more attuned to a higher purpose of your life.

34.

How Can We Prevent Suicides And What Are Your Thoughts About Assisted Mercy Killing Of A Person Who Is Incurably Ill?

Healing a death wish requires great support from all of us.

No one can prevent someone from committing suicide if he or she truly wants to die. Suicide is one of the most tragic things that people do to themselves. Depression, grief, and pain can be so insufferable that a person collapses into a heap of misery without escape. Society has suicide prevention centers with qualified people to come to the rescue of a person about to kill himself. We should make these centers accessible and have them staffed with the best people.

The sad thing about suicide is the finality of it. No matter how bleak a situation is to a depressed person, conditions can change in time. Somehow all hope and faith have evaporated from the minds of these people. If you ever experience a person who is thinking about suicide, listen to him, understand him, soothe him, and encourage him to be patient. Remind him that tomorrow is another day. There are rewards in life even when everything seems utterly desolate and inconsolable. There are ways to help a person restructure his life so he can begin a new journey down a healthy, life-affirming path.

The topic of assisted suicide for people whose lives are riddled with physical pain without cure is one of many mixed emotions for almost everyone. If an older man or woman diagnosed with a slow, debilitating, fatal disease—who possesses a keen, rational mind—wants to end his life instead of being thrown into the indignation of a brutal demise, then we are caught in a very tough dilemma. Does society permit suicide under special circumstances or does it uphold the principle that life is sacred and to aid another in suicide is murder? There are fine lines here. What happens if a cure is discovered soon after the death? Who is to say when it is permissible to help someone kill himself?

Under what extreme conditions? Will euthanasia become widespread? Will it go too far? Who will decide the difference between murder and assisted suicide?

These questions are difficult to answer. My personal opinion is we need to proceed very carefully with this subject. If a person is suffering and does not want to live and there are no cures, who are we to force him into an unendurable, prolonged death march? If all immediate family members support his decision to die, then his decision should be honored. How this should be carried out is also unclear and full of loopholes. This subject needs the attention of professional people who understand the ramifications well. All of us should not run from this subject; we should start a discussion with our friends to get more insights. We need to explore how we feel and what we ourselves would do in these dire circumstances. Clarity will come to us in time.

35.

Why Do People Lie?

We must teach a person who lies how the truth can be a liberation from fear.

There has always been a portion of people alive in every society who acted in opposition to the values most of us try to live by and honor. Some social scientists and anthropologists seem to think our DNA has a degree of bad genes propelling some of us to perpetrate terrible things upon others. This is impossible to quantify so I will not explore the genetic aspect of the subject.

A person lies to get his way. He uses a lie to manipulate other people to try to control the outcome of a given situation. Lying to others is a way to push yourself into a direction you want to go. It is, in essence, a use of trickery to outsmart or out maneuver another person for your personal advantage. People do this because they feel it is a necessary method in order to achieve their objective. They do it out of disregard for others. They lie to get empowerment and leverage over others.

Most of the time a person feels no guilt about lying. He thinks he has no choice but to lie in order to get something he wants. Lies can manifest in all kinds of situations. A man can lie to a woman he is first dating to lure her into having sex with him. A student can lie to his teacher about losing his homework when he never did it. A woman can lie to a friend because she wants this friend to like her. People can lie to everyone just to feel safe in the world. They can exaggerate information about themselves to boost their feelings of self-worth. They embellish facts to place themselves in certain favors with others. They lie about money; possessions; beliefs and their history just to elicit certain reactions in another person. Sometimes lies take precedence to such an extent the person begins to believe his own lies are true.

In our complex world it seems that lying has become an unavoidable behavioral tactic we have no choice but to rely upon in difficult sets of circumstances.

Let's go deeper into the dynamic of lying. Integrity and authenticity are values we hold in high esteem. No one wants to be perceived as a liar! No one feels good about having to lie his or her way through life. Lying is against the natural flow of who we are as a species. It hurts us in the end, weakening our resolve to feel free. It does this because it puts bars (metaphorically) around us, keeping us a prisoner to the false information we have offered the world and ourselves! Lying is a curse because it drains us of our life force.

When we can reach a place of inner safety and security, lying to others is completely contrary to our true self. Honesty is the best way to lead us to meaningful connections with others. Honesty is a doorway we can walk through to lead us to the place inside ourselves where the air we breathe is pure and the ground we stand upon is solid and supportive. It is in this place we can begin to trust life and trust others because we now trust ourselves. Being transparent is refreshing and revitalizing. It actually aids us in getting closer to the mystical spirit residing within us. It leads us to the center of joy.

People respect others who are honest. They trust them and respond in honest ways themselves. We create our reality to be one of clarity and wonder by holding up the torch of honesty. There is no need to lie because our intentions and our beliefs are clear to others and to us.

If you are a person who has wielded lies most of your life, you need to realign your system of functioning with a new order. Find the power in honesty. Find the freedom in honesty. Your lying has woven a suffocating straightjacket around your soul. Remove it by being honest, by refusing to continue on the path of deception and denial. Once you start to remove your straightjacket, your body, your mind and your heart will be reborn with a new lightness. You will begin to smile upon the world when, in the past, you lived in a state of suspicion and fear.

Honesty will unfurl new sails in your ship where you can visit new islands of beauty and serenity. These islands will nurture and revive you. Meet them with your higher self. The rewards awaiting you are immeasurable!

36.

Why Is There So Much Sexual Exploitation Of Women And Why Are There Many Sexual Issues Between Men And Women?

Men and women need to begin the process of understanding and respecting each other's sexuality.

There are multiple factors to this subject requiring extensive examination. I will, for the sake of brevity, touch upon a few of them by getting to the essence of my thoughts. Much of what I cover will be based on generalizations; there are obviously exceptions to every conclusion I draw.

Exploitation of women is widespread in many cultures in modern times. Men can use women to stimulate their libidos and to excite their fantasies. Men have a strong, innate sexual energy. The misuse of this can create a pervasive exploitation of women, using them as a magnetic appeal to sell homes, cars, food, clothing and a vast array of other material goods needed or not needed by people. Some men objectify women for their own personal thrills. Cultures that suppress women totally by restricting their freedom and forcing them to cover their bodies and faces indulge in male-dominated forms of abuse.

Conscious men want to bond with a woman, communicate deeply and want the assurance of acceptance through sexuality and intimacy. The interaction between a man and a woman in a romantic context is often simultaneously exhilarating yet dramatic. Women are buoyed by friendship and the power of close communication. The sexual dynamic between the sexes is a complex, intricate dance of emotions, passion, and understanding.

Sex mixed with emotional love is an incomparable, powerful energy. Men and women need to discover what forces are compelling them to interact sexually— rather than the obvious force of libido. Sexuality is, of course, the most primal of energies on the physical level because it is the necessary action that will perpetuate our species and express deep love.

Since we have evolved from the stages of lust in the early period of our evolution as Homo sapiens, we have been influenced by a higher consciousness around sexuality. Today, there are the energies of compassion, pleasing, trusting, caring, nurturing, cherishing and honoring the sacredness of love through the dance of the body.

Men and women need to be discerning with their sexuality. They need to understand themselves well in order to give and receive sexual love. Whatever schisms exist can be removed through understanding, patience, sensitivity and appreciation for the differences between the two sexes.

Men and women need to revolutionize their way of perceiving, treating and interacting with each other sexually. Knowledge of each other will help narrow the gap that has existed between the sexes for centuries. It will allow for a clearer communication between a man and a woman. It provides empathy that will enable them to harmonize together and open their hearts in unprecedented ways. Men need women and women need men. We are on the brink of a new paradigm of relationships between the sexes. It will take a massive

effort on both men's and women's part to heal the past
hurts and disappointments so both sexes can experience
joy and beauty in the expression of themselves through
their sexuality. Love reaches its zenith in the sexual
merger of a man and a woman. And through this love,
the world can become a happier and more peaceful place.

37.

Why Are There Such Problems Of Wealth And Poverty Among Humans?

The solution to all poverty is for each of us to incorporate an attitude of fairness and care, for no one should be left behind in the distribution of wealth.

This subject has been reverberating down the corridors of civilizations for centuries. It is a huge predicament! There has always been the struggle of the ones with the majority of wealth against those who scrape along at the lower end. There's no question this problem exists at all levels of society—even among family and individual relationships. Successfully distributing the wealth equitably has never worked.

There is duality in this world; there is avarice; there is jealousy; there is suffering; there is unfairness! No doubt these realities enervate our collective movement toward a healthier, more vibrant society for the whole of humanity. No doubt these things crush the spirits of those mired in poverty and deprivation.

There is no simple solution. Yet we can, as individuals, raise the level of our awareness and act in concert with a higher, more compassionate manner toward all people. Rather than lament about these conditions, let us strive to be more sympathetic toward the people who don't have much material comfort. Let us not condemn those who gravitate toward luxury and opulence. Instead, let us try our best to educate the masses one person at a time to remember that if one individual goes hungry or if one person is bereft of hope, home or the basic necessities then it is incumbent upon the rest of us to try our best to heal this situation.

No one person is separate from the family of humanity. No one person, clinging to the fringes of the garden of plenty waiting for scraps to keep him alive, should be excluded from the bounty of our harvest. No one should be pushed out into the streets to fend for himself in the brutal insensitivity of our rejection!

We are all brothers and sisters trying to manage as we bounce around the infrastructures of societies rewarding the strong and clever. Those who have struggled to fit in are no more undeserving than the most influential potentate among us. There are a few individuals—who somehow command tremendous attention because of their wealth, their flaunting egos and their lust for power—who are no more valuable than the wretched soul of a homeless man whose past wounds of suffering have plunged him into a life of resignation on the streets.

Be part of the solution. Live a virtuous life yourself. Be an example of what you feel is the right way to live. Don't scorn those who have wealth. Rather stand up for what you know in your heart is the best way to treat every single man, woman and child you encounter as you make your way through diverse landscapes of human culture. Be a shining example of a virtuous person by demonstrating your compassion and generosity. Let others experience the wisdom of your love for your fellow humans. This is the greatest gift you can offer! Be a beacon of light to the world by living each day in sacred appreciation of all beings!

38.

What Can We Do With The Elderly Who Are Unable To Care For Themselves?

*When we band together to serve the elderly
we are helping to heal the world.*

The last phase of a person's long life is often extremely difficult. The body and mind don't function as well and the individual may be unable to take care of himself. It is an unspeakable challenge for the rest of us to watch the deterioration of the elderly. Society has failed terribly in solving this problem. Yes, it can be solved. Despite the massive necessity to correct this affair, we as a society have not confronted this prevalent issue; we have chosen to ignore it, shoving it under the rug of our denial.

142

The solution is simple. We need to make elder care a top priority for every person in our nation. We need to set up systems that provide the best care for the needy. There should be beautiful facilities for the elderly that are designed to make them as comfortable as humanly possible. These facilities should be like resorts with the best medical, emotional, and spiritual services available to everyone. Private rooms lavishly decorated; classical music; shows and entertainment; activities of a great assortment; alternative medical treatments; delectable cuisine and counseling are some of the necessary infrastructures needed for a comfortable situation in the last phase of a person's life.

Who should pay for the exorbitant cost of maintaining these facilities? Society. All of us must contribute to this vital cause throughout our lives. We need to pay for the care of our elderly through taxes. We need to make sacrifices for the sake of treating those people unable to care for themselves with dignity, comfort, and compassion. When we do this, we honor the journey of life for those who leave their incredible legacy.

39.

What Are Your Thoughts About Hunting?

No one creature, no matter how small or large, is less precious than a human being.

People kill wild boar in the forests. They shoot wolves from helicopters. They take down huge brown bears with powerful rifles. They harpoon whales. They spear seals and club baby seals with their mothers wailing in agony beside them. They shoot squirrels, pull marlin from the ocean, and obliterate elephants, tigers, lions and crocodiles in the wild.

I worship the beasts of the Earth. They are my brothers and sisters. I see them as more advanced than I am because they live closer to the raw essence of life.

144

They are masters of their worlds. They seek nothing more than to live, to eat and to raise their young—and they experience a complete oneness of life in these cycles. They are the progeny of Nature. We should learn from them; we should cherish them. At worst case, we should leave them alone and allow them to follow their own destinies without our cruelty and intrusions.

Instead of hunting them, send them love; send them your blessings. Respect the boundaries they need in the privacy of their existence. We don't welcome them in our cities; we should not enter their environments unless it is for an excellent reason to help them as a last resort. They are not asking to coalesce with us. They are perfect without us. When we honor this truth we are giving ourselves the gift of living in peace with Nature's miraculous creatures. Our survival has nothing to do with killing animals. This was necessary thousands of years ago.

Let us come together in mutual respect. Let us remember how the beasts bring energy and magic to the world. Let us send out our prayers asking not for forgiveness—for grudges do not exist in the world of animals—but for their safety so that all of us are comforted by the success of our survival as we make our way into the mystical future.

40.

What Can Be Done To Make Public Schools Better Educational Institutions?

When we teach young people how to cultivate good values and virtues, we are investing in a healthy future for civilization.

The time a young person spends at school from around age five to eighteen is enormous. Throughout his or her developmental stages, a young person is exposed to an array of ideas and social interactions. In our society we focus mainly upon educating a young person with information and facts that require an adept memory. This is very limited. What needs to be demonstrated and reinforced throughout the entire span of education is character building. Teach young people about ethics. Teach them about compassion. Teach them about resolving conflicts with their peers.

Teach them about inner strength and confidence. Teach them about the infinite reservoir living within them upon which they can build the mantle and mettle of their true nature. Teach them about the art of living in gratitude and joy. Teach them about contributing to society. Teach them about the sacredness of life. When you do these things in a world bristling with anger, despair and struggle, you help a young person create a destiny abounding with beauty, peace and love.

41.

Should Abortions Be Allowed?

Every woman must have sovereignty over her life.

All life is sacred. Certainly the conception of a human infant is a miracle unto itself. Taking life in its embryonic stage is something all of us dread. The solution to this problem of unwanted pregnancy has answers. Educate women and men about procreation, especially about the pros and cons of contraceptives. We need to make sure everyone has access to this information and the devices that prevent pregnancy. If, for reasons beyond the control of the couple, the woman accidently gets pregnant, we need to inform her about the available options. Adoption and the possibility of actually changing her mind and her wanting to have her child must be carefully presented to her.

After all choices are clearly explained and understood, the final choice is up to the woman herself. If she unambiguously does not want to bring the baby into the world and does not want to give it up for adoption, then the final decision is ultimately hers. Abortion should be made available as a last resort to the pregnant woman. In a world with millions of unwanted children, we cannot force a woman to bring another child here if she adamantly does not want to proceed with her pregnancy. A woman has to have sovereignty over her body and her destiny.

42.

Why Do Some Government Leaders Become Corrupt With Their Power?

We need to create a new form of selecting our leaders, one based upon merit—not power.

Most leaders are high achievers who aspire to command authority over others. These people come from the mold that breeds strong-willed, assertive, demonstrative and outgoing personalities. They are people who know how to ingratiate themselves in the good graces of others who will eventually yield their own power to the stronger leader. Once a person with these characteristics gains a momentum of authority, it is difficult to stop. He or she is tempted by the constant allure of more power. They get caught in an increasingly intense spiral.

The people who come from the mold of treating everyone fairly, and who don't believe in taking charge of other people's lives, seldom seek leadership positions. These magnanimous souls don't want to rise to the top of the pedestal and proclaim dominion over the masses. They don't want the attention, fame and glory.

There have been some stellar leaders throughout history who dedicated their lives to serving humanity by espousing the highest ideals for everyone. These few leaders inspired millions by the causes they championed, leaving profound changes in their wake.

Most people who strive to be the leaders are, by their inherent nature, prone to the seduction of power. It is an unfortunate dilemma for the nations of the world. It is a very rare individual who manages to gain political triumph and still maintain his common self. It takes an almost inhuman effort for a person in charge of millions not to find himself swept into the despotic riptides his position invariably produces. Hubris, immunity from justice and the adoration of his minions create the perfect ingredients for a leader corrupted by power.

In an advanced society, a person should earn a leadership position through the meritorious legacy of his past deeds. An eclectic group of people needs to be represented by individuals who genuinely want to lead them to a place of stability, prosperity and equality.

43.

Why Do So Many People Struggle With Work?

The work world needs a major transformation where everyone feels good about careers.

I n this age of civilization, when the pressures to survive and to advance materially are ever-present, many people find themselves inextricably trapped in a working situation that has become a form of enslavement. We live in a society that demands productivity, requiring a person to sacrifice his own personal needs and goals for the benefit of the company. The workweek is often a period of duress, consuming a person's life.

The typical work system tries to make robots out of most of us. This system weakens our love of life and restricts the natural predilection to be creative. No wonder many of us either drink, smoke, take drugs, act neurotically or disdain the mundane lives to which we have succumbed. This is an unfortunate commentary of what we have become as a collective group of individuals comprising a functioning society.

We have forged a huge empire of material glorification requiring incessant diligence in order to sustain itself. This empire is predicated upon a constant state of insatiability. The more we want something, the more we need to produce it. This dynamic is a spiraling funnel into which we are all falling deeper and deeper. The rich want to get richer, while the poor and middle class find themselves mired deeper in a malaise, which exacerbates their insecurities and fears of being destitute.

This does not have to exist. We don't have to suffer implacably in a system that is not conscious, not humanitarian, not loving, not spiritually healthy.

The solution is simple, although not easy to implement. The work world needs to be completely revamped, making it compatible with the needs of the very people who fuel it. Workers need to be treated much more kindly and compassionately. They need to be respected and honored for the immense contribution they make in providing our society with all the goods we own.

Oppressive conditions, low compensation and the threat of termination only act as a hindrance to morale and efficient productivity. No one wants to feel enslaved, trapped and walking on a tightrope, terrified of falling into the abyss of unemployment. The more you inspire a worker, the more likely he or she will want to perform at the highest level. Encouragement is one of the strongest, most potent motivators. Somehow the people in charge have forgotten this fact or else they are too insecure themselves to allow for more compassionate and respectful treatment of the workers who answer to them.

Another important aspect to the transformative, healing modality of work is that of teamwork. When people work together in cooperation, unified and utilizing each other's best skills, amazing things can happen. Creativity is ignited; people feel as though they are part of a team. The team energy, when it is galvanized by the people's enthusiasm and positivity, is a powerhouse of creativity that cannot be throttled by outside interference. The work world needs a complete reversal of how it treats its workers. This change will win the hearts of countless people whose attitudes have been apathetic and compromised.

Additionally, the workweek needs to become humane and conducive for people. The typical eight-hour day should be reduced to five hours. The five-day week should become four days. Shorter hours will encourage people to become more focused and more productive. Time off from work will aid in balancing a person's life. Everyone needs ample time to fulfill other activities and to experience a respite from the arduous tasks of work. This concept is imperative for a healthy, more robust output of energy by workers of the world.

Then, of course, there is the subject of compensation. Capitalism is fundamentally designed to minimize wages to the workers while maximizing profits. This will not work forever. This will not serve everyone. It reeks of blatant exploitation and oppression. A humane ingredient needs to be added to the capitalistic formula—fairness! Pay people well for a job well done. Invest in your workers and their loyalty and devotion will strengthen. Distribute the profits in a more equitable manner. Then everyone will feel better and prosper. Then the economic engine will flourish more successfully than when a disproportionate number of people benefit.

We have a choice to determine our destiny, both as individuals and as an aggregate system of people aspiring to the same goal. This goal is joy. It is freedom. It is security. But we cannot achieve security alone.

Although many of us operate as if we were independent of the other people around us, we are all truly connected. We cannot separate ourselves from the strife our fellow humans endure daily. We want to be oblivious to them. We want to ignore their cries by rationalizing that there is nothing we as individuals can do. We want to shut our eyes to the suffering of animals, or the destruction of whole ecosystems. We resign ourselves to thinking we are powerless to do anything about these problems. We think the only course of action is to take care of ourselves. We keep strengthening our own bastion of protection, our own position that keeps us safe and impervious to the suffering of the outside world. This is a huge misconception.

What happens to one of us impacts the entire species. We need to come together to tackle the problems besetting the world. We need to embrace our humanity to realize our oneness and our magnificence. Our evolution is synonymous with change. The change that is unfolding at this very moment is augmenting our chances for survival. We must not resist it. We must breathe energy into it with our courage, hope and unyielding compassion for all life on Earth!

SECTION THREE

The World & Nature

There's no doubt that we live in a world that is highly diversified and complex. We have a tendency to impose limited values on subjects we cannot explain and understand. In this section the subjects are presented in clear and objective ways to give us greater clarity how they interact with us. We learn how to develop more reverence for the mystery of life and how to make peace with things that have puzzled us in the past.

44.

Are Animals As Evolved As We Are And Do They Have Souls?

Every sentient being has a soul.

If one approaches this question from a purely anatomical perspective, animals are much more evolved than humans. In most climates we would perish, without clothes, from the elements and the cold. Many animals and birds can endure much more cold and much more heat than we can. Animals can swim to depths of thousands of feet in the ocean and hold their breaths thirty times longer than we can hold ours. Some species of mammals can run two to three times faster; leap much farther than we can; jump much higher; survive droughts for weeks and even months; go without eating for months; have no water for weeks.

Birds can fly as high as jet airplanes and dive at over two hundred miles per hour. Some species can change the color of their skin and some can even change their actual sex. Some can sleep for six months without food or water. Should I include the insect world? The list would last for pages. Let me mention just one of them: an insect thought to be dead for many years in a university laboratory was able to resurrect itself with some water and sunlight! I think animals are much more evolved than we are in many ways.

Now let me touch upon the facets that are not measurable. Their personalities and their behaviors seem much more tuned in to the rhythms of the Earth. They don't harm the natural world—as a matter of fact they hardly change their environments. They don't leave in their wakes a huge mess causing ecological ruination. They don't conspire together to take over the world or to eliminate other species. They don't go on a destructive rampage and they don't deplete their food sources by mismanaging the distribution.

The creatures of the Earth seem much more content than we are. They seem at peace with their destinies and accept the conditions of their lives. They don't resign themselves to failure or moan about their existence. They seem closer to the divine by how grateful they are for the simplest of activities such as a leaf to eat, a mound to roll around on, a stream from which to drink, and the smell of wet grass.

Animals are certainly as evolved as we are, only differently, and have much to teach us just by the way they live. Do they have souls? If we have souls, they have souls. A grasshopper has one; a worm has one; a flea has one; a hawk has one; an eel has one. All living things were spawned out of the same force and all of them are like threads of beauty woven into the divine tapestry of life.

45.

How Can We Find Peace With Aging?

Aging is a time to go inward to discover the deepest meaning to life.

Aging is a pervasive issue everyone must face. The truth is, we began aging the moment we were conceived. Aging is an immutable process of Nature that every living thing experiences. For humans, it is easy to age for the first fifty or so years because our bodies remain strong, robust and healthy.

For all people a discernible physical change happens past fifty and certainly past sixty years of life. This change embodies a vast slew of obvious transformations none of us desire. The body prepares itself for the inevitable death throes that take place

162

over any period of a few years to many years. Skin deteriorates; eyes weaken; limbs ache; hearing fails; muscles atrophy; organs stop performing well and the brain loses its acuity. The older we become the more pronounced these failings are. It is the destiny of all life.

It is not easy to admonish a person in his or her nineties about having a positive attitude as his body slips into painful disarray. It is not easy to ask a person to ignore the struggles and challenges of a body refusing to perform at a level that makes walking, eating and sleeping effortless. Aging is a rough road, indeed.

Aging is a harsh reality. We can't dismiss or pretend it doesn't exist. It happens at different levels to different people. All of us will die before long. A hundred years is rare, and a hundred and twenty years is almost impossible. Death of the body started a long time ago and was wired into our DNA in our genes.

With all this said, there is still a way to manage aging by reducing the enormity of difficulty. Accepting. Surrendering. Allowing. Appreciating the natural process without condemning it or resisting it. Go deep within to the quiet sanctuary of the soul and find peace with the solitude of your life. Give up the illusion of living beyond the natural gift given to you. Watch the world slip away because your body is unable to dance with life in ways that make the experience pleasurable. Smile at this powerful process. Despite the severity of it as it seizes your body and takes it away slowly, you are still free in your mind and heart. You are free to be the witness of your death that will lead you back into the formless, the eternal.

Old age is a time to take stock of one's life, to reminisce, to transcend and to awaken to a more profound spiritual understanding. It is a time to immerse yourself into creative endeavors such as painting, volunteering, writing, or supporting a worthy cause.

Be brave as your body loses its place among the strong and the young. Be courageous as you slide unwaveringly into the folds of the ultimate frontier. Don't be weakened by your body's decline in your resolve to broaden and enrich your feelings of oneness with something greater than the ephemeral journey you have lived. These ideas might seem esoteric and idealistic. They are. They are also potent forms of salvaging old age and bringing glimmers of light to a dismal situation. Never let your light dim! Never let the child in you stop singing its appreciation and its joy in silent exaltation to the world. You have been blessed to have lived a long life. Make room for others, for the long and mysterious parade of humanity marches steadily into the future.

46.

Do Advanced Life Forms Exist In The Universe And Can We Contact Them?

Life is abundant throughout the Universe—
finding it is the challenge.

The Universe is so vast it staggers our minds. There are over a hundred billion stars in our single galaxy alone. Remember, every star is a sun with varied sizes and temperatures, etc. There are billions of galaxies in the known Universe and each one has billions of suns. It is most likely true that every sun in the entire Universe has a multitude of planets revolving around them. The answer to your question is absolutely yes! The Universe teems with

165

life in such varied forms our imaginations cannot begin to speculate what these life forms are like.

We haven't yet detected life out in the fathomless Universe. We can't prove it is there so we approach the subject with our own subjective and presumptuous conclusions. We say we don't know. This is absurd. How dare we think that our speck in space is the only planet with life on it!

Science, in all its acclaim and capabilities, tries to decipher the mystery of things in the firmament by using empirical evidence to prove or disprove its hypotheses. This approach, although useful for many applications here on Earth, has little effectiveness for understanding the phenomena of the heavens.

Advanced life in the Universe is so prolific it would shock our minds. But don't get too excited by this because the chances of contacting any one of these extraterrestrial civilizations is next to impossible. The distances between the stars in our single galaxy are so great it is hard to conceive. Never mind the billions of other galaxies in the Universe. Traveling at the speed of light—a hundred and eighty six thousand miles per second—will take a continuous, direct trip hundreds, and in some cases thousands, of years to reach the other stars in our Milky Way Galaxy. This, of course, is just the time it would take to get there one way. Returning home will take twice as long.

Bluntly put, there are many things we cannot know about the nature of the Universe. We speculate about these phenomena all the time. We deduce theories that are somewhat substantiated by scientific inquiry. But the truth is we know practically nothing. I personally believe there are zillions of Universes being born and dying simultaneously every nanosecond. Universes collapse, implode into infinitesimal sizes, and then explode all over again to form new Universes. Time itself is a complex thing that applies to the illusion of one phase of existence. Life and death may be a flicker of one of the infinite changes taking place all at once on an endless cycle of fantastic transformations.

The human brain cannot penetrate the innumerable other dimensions beyond the three-dimensional world we relate to in our daily lives. It is best to look up at the stars, smiling with a sense of glee and awe, for you and I and everything else in all existence are an inextricable part of the kaleidoscopic dance of the Cosmos!

47.

How Do Animals Heal People?

The animals who inhabit the world with us often possess access to realms of intuition that can help restore and heal their masters' lives.

Animals live in a different dimension of life than we humans do. They operate in spheres of invisible places where their instincts can pick up imperceptible vibrations in other animals. Animals function in a space of harmony with Nature. They do not attack unless they are hungry or they feel threatened in some way by an intruder. Their natural state is love—which I would characterize as contentment, peace, and appreciation for the moment. There is little discord in the animal world. Their minds are not beset with worry and fear plaguing humans such as uncertainty about the future.

The animals that have assimilated well into our world feel us on deep levels, sensing when we are out of rhythm with ourselves. Their instinctive reaction is to come to our aid, to rescue us, to help heal us. Within them is a maternal instinct that knows how to send out healing waves of energy. How they do this remains a mystery. Perhaps it is an irrepressible urge to encourage members of the animal's intimate family to regain their strength. Whatever it is, there is a raw power in the animal's capacity to recharge a sick person's body. They do this with an unremitting focus by projecting a sweet energy. They do it by their intention, which is brimming with love, care, and compassion.

We can learn a powerful axiom from these animals. By giving to another person who is in need of a friend benefits the whole world. For life ever seeks to lift itself to higher ground where the experience for all is a magnificent event!

48.

How Can We Help
Save The Earth?

*Every nation and every person must adopt a
program to help heal the planet.*

The Earth is the womb to countless life forms. It sustains every one of them through the transmutations of geological time. Because of our great minds and our ability to influence the physical world to a huge extent, humans are the stewards of the Earth. Yet, at the same time, we have plundered the Earth, causing irreparable damage. In modern times since the industrial revolution, we have left in our wake a trail of pollution of the most odious kind. This is serious business. Destroying the ecosystems of the planet—whether the air, soil, forests, rivers, lakes and oceans—creates catastrophic consequences!

Things are bleak, for sure. The world is teetering over an abyss into which many species could fall within our lifetime. We are all threatened by the ominous facts of the planet heating up and environmental degradation looming in the imminent future.

I do, however, believe we can save our planet if we put our focus on it. It will take a massive campaign on the part of every nation and every person in the world. It will take an unprecedented action of unyielding devotion to possibly reverse the state of the world. The first thing that needs to happen is to reduce the number of people from over seven billion to one billion. This is an extraordinary objective, indeed. It will require everyone's cooperation. Bringing children into the world will require couples to get prior approval from their community organization whose function is to monitor human population. Once the current generation gets old and dies of natural causes, the next generation will be forced to maintain the number of offspring it can produce. Then the next generation will have further restrictions until the population of humans on Earth will be fixed around one billion people.

It's obvious that the number of one billion down from seven billion will have one-seventh the amount of harm we can cause to the Earth. But there is another factor essential to transforming our planet into a healthy one. It is educating and mandating everyone to become a zealous proponent of living in the green zone. This means we as a species treat all other species with reverence. We greatly limit what we take from the Earth's resources. We change our lifestyles to a natural one where we use less water, less wood, less fuel, less energy. We develop systems of transportation that are safe and environmentally supportive. We change our diets to a plant based one. We treat every stream, river, lake and ocean with great care, making sure they remain pristine and unpolluted.

We change our entire consciousness to worship the land, the animals, the air and water as living embodiments of the same spirit of which we are all made. With this new paradigm of thinking and behaving, our civilizations will be in synch with the natural rhythms of the Earth and we will not be a detrimental force interfering with the evolution of life.

The question at hand is practicality. You might say, "This sounds great in theory but in reality it is impossible to achieve." You are probably correct in thinking this way. It is an insurmountable task to get the disparate nations of the world to agree to such a stringent plan—let alone follow it.

But the question does ask how we can help save the world. The truth is we have no choice but to make drastic changes. If we don't practice these on our own, Nature will inevitably force us to make changes. If we are to survive as a species living on this amazing planet, we will need to put into practice a way of life that will work harmoniously with the Earth in allowing us to continue into the folds of a wonderful future.

49.

How Do We Heal Our Bodies?

Your body is a masterpiece created by Nature, and it is your responsibility to cherish it.

It is a wondrous blessing to have been given the gift of a body. The one thing remaining with you your entire life is your body. This is your temple; it is the instrument through which you play the music of your soul. It needs to be loved and cared for; it needs to be adored and fine-tuned. Maintaining the body is wired into your brain from eons of wading through the challenges of survival. Built into your being are the memory codes that demand vigilant care and protection of your body.

You are the culmination of inestimable forces designing you out of the elements of the Earth. You are the heir to the triumphs of countless generations that have lived before you who passed on their genes to help form the body you own today.

How you treat your body is a reflection of how you respect yourself. The sole function of the body is to make the ride through life as comfortable, pleasant and joyous as possible. Nature formed you out of exquisite elements. Your body is your ship. You are its captain and its crew. You are the engine and the rudder. Your inner self has created whatever happens to your body on some arcane level. Your outlook on life affects your ship. How you sailed your ship through tempests and harsh conditions determines the healthy state it finds itself. Your body is not a neutral system. It loves you. It is you. But you must love it back tenfold.

You must cherish it and take excellent care of it. Feed it great food; nurture it; give it ample rest; exercise it; soothe it and treat it to special experiences.

If you are sick, you are out of balance and need to realign your energy. If you experience your body as a burden and a curse, you need to examine how you feel about life and then sort out the poisonous beliefs and replace them with healthy ones.

Taking care of the body requires time, energy and devotion. You know the right thing to do for your body. The answers are made evident for everyone to know. Treat your body as if it were your best friend in life. When you take a walk, be conscious of the amazing synchronicity of your feet and legs. Love the fragrances drifting into your nostrils. Feel the breeze caressing your face. Say to yourself in silence: "I feel wonderful and I honor my body for the glorious experience of walking upon the lovely Earth or through this city. This is a temporary gift and I thank life for this fantastic experience allowing me to know the material world through the senses of my body. I am blessed."

50.

Why Do Some People Cheat and Steal?

These aberrant behaviors can be unlearned when good morality and consciousness are introduced.

People who cheat and do unethical things to gain something for themselves are operating in a narrow space of serving only themselves. They feel the only way to get what they want is by cheating. This form of behavior comes from an extreme position of separation from other people. The individual feels limited by his own resourcefulness so he or she uses cheating to get what he wants. This person has little faith and confidence in himself, and feels that he has no choice but to cheat in order to prevail successfully.

But there is another element to this subject that is rarely brought to the surface. Cheating is a manifestation on the part of the person that comes from a deep-rooted anger at the world for causing him frustrations and disappointments throughout his lifetime. Cheating the system or another person is a form of retribution, getting back at the world for years of failure and abuse. It is a blame game where the person gets to win by using his anger and disregard for the laws of the land. He is throwing daggers at the world without getting caught—so he thinks.

The person who cheats is setting himself up for getting caught. He is making himself vulnerable to repercussions. This does not stop the cheater from carrying out his actions. The cheater's insecurities will compel him to do whatever it takes to control the desired outcome he wants to see come to fruition.

Healing the person who cheats requires a complete reframing of his way of thinking and his concept of life. It will require a rewiring of his values by taking away the attention on him by beginning to perceive other people as belonging to the family of life. He will need to stop blaming the world for his failures by taking responsibility for his own destiny. And most importantly, he will need to confront the lifetime accumulation of anger and lance this abscessed, poisonous defect until there is practically nothing left. Although his anger can be justified at times, he must be willing to transcend it, jettisoning it out of his thoughts and body. This is the only way he can gain a sense of security about himself and, at the same time, feel in harmony with the rest of the world.

Stealing is an action of extreme selfishness and disregard for another person or organization from which he steals. When a person steals he is acting out a form of abuse by taking what does not belong to him. Stealing comes from a limited and contracted consciousness that does not care about others. The people who steal justify their actions by telling themselves they have a right to take what does not belong to them. They believe the people who have the goods they want don't deserve them or should share these goods with others.

When a person steals a package left by the front door of a person's home—without even knowing what is inside the package—he is making a statement that says: "Give me your gift because you don't deserve it! I want what you have! I am more important than you are! I don't give a damn what you think or feel when you lose your package!" The thief who steals separates himself from the person from whom he is taking the package. In essence, a thief dehumanizes his victims by dismissing their pain his theft causes. He gloats about his victory at getting away with the crime and pats himself on the back for a job well done.

The mindset of the thief is rife with poisonous thoughts. The thief feels the world owes him things for free because of the rough journey of deprivation he has had to endure since childhood.

Healing the thief requires a prodigious self-journey to unravel the complexity of values living inside him. He needs to return to society as a caring, responsible and appreciative person. In order to achieve this new consciousness, he must undergo a complete reframing of who he is. He must awaken to something that has escaped him most of his life: empathy. This starts by learning how to feel what others feel. It requires getting out of the way of the self by focusing on other people. Managing this new system of thinking will require a one-dimensional discipline to develop a love of humanity.

The only way a thief can reverse his modality of behavior is to learn to love people. When you love and respect others, it is very difficult to hurt them by stealing their possessions or their money. Love others as belonging to the same family as you, and your experience of life will provide you with a profound sense of joy and fulfillment.

51.

Why Is There So Much Violence In The World?

We have a choice how we want to live and what we allow into our lives.

There is violence in Nature. Violence does permeate much of the natural world. But I will focus on human violence and how it impacts our own species as well as others.

Human beings have been tremendously violent in countless ways. We slaughter and eat billions of animals, birds and fish every year! We attack each other in moments of rage. We form together with like-minded individuals, using our best ingenious resources, to wage war against other groups of people.

We hunt for sport. We use violence to wield power over others for many reasons. We seek retribution against those whom we perceive have wronged us. We make weapons capable of annihilating entire cities. As a species, we are steeped in violence to the point that our entertainment explodes with it and even the toys we give our children are often replications of violent weapons!

Is there a way out of the violent madness? Yes, there is a way to stop the flood of violence by making a choice not to participate in this arena. Each person is the architect of his or her destiny and each one of us can become conscious of the ways we react to upsetting situations or to threats. Rage, hurt, fear, disgust, betrayal, and abandonment will happen to all of us at some time during our lives. What we do about them is the ultimate question of whether we help heal the conflict or inflame it; whether we escalate the problem or reconcile it; whether we engage in violence or live in peace.

Whatever energies and thoughts occur inside us will attract similar extrinsic energies. People playing with violent thoughts, or are besieged with worry about being attacked, become unwitting participants in the vortex of violence. Cultivate peaceful thoughts and feelings, live with peace emanating from your being, and peace will follow you wherever you go.

Watching violence, hearing about violence, reading about violence make us insensitive to its destructive force and in some ways pushes violence closer to us as we condone or excuse it. It is easy to justify violence by using numerous rationalizations. The human mind can easily ignore horrible things because the mind glosses over them with a coat of anesthetized beliefs. Genocide throughout history was successfully carried out because hoards of people allowed it to happen by passivity and their twisted beliefs.

Take a strong stand for peace. Be a champion of peace. Live your life in peace. Work every day to encourage others to join the march for peace. We can change our predisposition toward violence in how we think and how we respond to potential conflicts. Peace is a choice. It is a healthy one for each of us and for the rest of living things on planet Earth.

52.

Is There Anything I Can Personally Do To Make The World A Better Place?

Each one of us makes a difference in the world through our actions and lifestyle.

Yes, there is something you personally can do for the world. Start by taking immediate action in how you conduct yourself from moment to moment. You can't save the world but you sure can contribute toward its improvement in a huge way. Use the full power of your consciousness to make decisions that will make everyone around you a beneficiary.

Some of the examples of these decisions are: Be aware of your every word so that it conveys a positive, uplifting message to everyone with whom you talk, and make sure you smile at everyone you meet with a genuine glow emanating from you. If you can offer to help an elderly woman with her bags of groceries, do so as often as you can. Be conscientious of the Earth's energy you use by trying to limit it as much as possible. When you see a child in need, do everything you can to serve this child.

Wake up every morning with a feeling of glee and appreciation. Sing to the birds. Feed a stray cat. Offer to help the homeless. Give of yourself as freely as possible. Be generous with everyone. Do not scorn or discriminate against anyone because of the way he lives. Lead with compassion; spread the wealth of your enthusiasm wherever you go. Walk with your head high and strut with jubilation as you travel down the path of your life. But never show off or look down upon anyone. When you see a forlorn, broken person, make him feel good in your presence. Empathize with the downtrodden and then give them all the love within you.

Trust the world. Revere it. Believe in the universal dream of a world where everyone feels loved, appreciated, and safe. When you see a stranger weeping, turn to this person as if he were your best friend. Never take credit for the good deeds you perform, for each one is a gift of life working through you in honor of a higher, more sacred power.

Live from your heart where every person and every living thing you meet along the way is a gift for you to cherish. Hold high the torch of light in the darkest moments, for even the blind can be led to a brighter place.

Do these things and much more as natural, spontaneous expressions of who you are, and the world will move unwaveringly toward perfection. You are the intermediary between the ideal conditions we all strive to reach and the reality of experiencing them!

SECTION FOUR

Spirituality & Philosophy

Spiritual matters have always been controversial throughout history. Here we delve into the nature of spirituality to change the abstract into lucid meaning. We take the secrets that exist beyond the rational mind to make sense out of them. This grasp of the esoteric world will give us specific guidelines to lead us beyond the range of our present thinking into the essence of life's majesty and wonder.

53.

What Is A Realistic And Simple Formula To Living A Happy Life?

Everyone can be happy by readjusting attitudes and perspectives.

Tell yourself you will honor and worship who you are at all times. You will be the caretaker of yourself, providing a sense of wellness and safety as you make your way through the world. In other words, you will have a blast with yourself. No one can love you the way you love yourself. I am not alluding to the love that is fostered by the ego, demanding attention and asserting its way over other people. The love of self I am referring to is so beautiful it bursts inside you like a beam of ecstatic light filling you with the rapture of life!

Once you know this self-love, you can follow the magical path wherever it takes you to a place called happiness.

The other major component to the formula of happiness is to unscrew the tight bolts holding you to the expectations you impose on others. This dynamic will invariably keep you in a frustrated and diminished place that compromises your love of life. You may never get people to follow you along the journey of your expectations. Accept the outside for what it is and flow with the currents of life. If no one joins you in your dance, then dance wildly by yourself. When you allow the world to unfold without your tampering with it, you will fly joyously in the ethers of a freedom no one can ever take away from you.

Another part of the formula is to not expect too much from yourself. You can strive for improvement and you can ascend the mountains of your dreams—but don't wait until you find the rainbow to exult in the perfection of the now. Have fun with yourself; laugh; play; celebrate the gift of life.

The last part of the formula to living a happy life is to give of your gifts, unconditionally. You possess a vast storehouse of special gifts. Spread them everywhere you go. It doesn't matter if others thank you or even receive your gifts. Just go on giving with gratitude and appreciation and you will bubble inside with happiness. At the moment you exit from this world, the remaining questions you will face are: "Did I live a happy life? Was I delighted at being me? Did I follow my destiny with all the joy and gusto in my soul?"

Your happiness is your own responsibility. It can be achieved with a strong set of beliefs and desires. It requires an ardent devotion on your part to follow your dreams without digressing and without allowing others to impede your natural inclination. Happiness is your birthright. Just because our parents or past generations struggled and didn't experience much happiness has nothing to do with our destiny. Happiness is an energy that will help heal you and will set you free to journey to magnificent places inside you and in the world!

54.

What Is The Nature Of Traditional Religions?

The one religion that transcends them all is the religion of unconditional love.

M ost traditional religions today are remnants of fanatical organizations from ancient times whose survival was predicated on convincing their followers of fantastically imagined stories that were meant to be taken as fact and true.

A great religion is one that has no doctrines; does not erect extravagant houses of worship; does not demand conformity; never intimidates with threats of condemnation and punishment; will not insist on converting everyone into believing the same story. A great religion dissolves and ultimately disappears in the power of life itself.

The lord of the Cosmos lives in you and in me...as well as an ant, a flower and a mountain. There is no holier place than where we stand right now. There is nothing more phantasmagorical and divine than the next breath we take. This is the only miracle—a palpable, dimensional, mystical fact that allows us an awareness of the wondrous, exploding, wild, ecstatic, inexplicable, living body of creation enraptured with itself! This is a religion that cannot be named or defined. It is the perpetual sacredness to which all of us belong—unconditional love.

55.

With All The Tumult Around Us, How Can We Have Inner, Lasting Peace?

Achieving inner peace requires self-discipline and focus.

Step outside of the external world by taking a deep breath, close your eyes, relax and what do you see? You see your thoughts or perhaps you see nothing. Invite tranquility into the moment. Keep breathing and become aware of your body. Don't judge anything. Just be with yourself. Try to remove the elements of time from the moment. Your thoughts keep racing. This is because you live in your mind and it doesn't want to release control over you. Your thoughts are not you. They are images and feelings you conjure from the vast storehouse of ideas, fears and beliefs you have acquired and cultivated over your lifetime. Your inner world is empty. It is separate from the outside world.

If you truly want peace you need to shut off the continuous stream of thoughts floating around in your mind. They have no importance to the moment when you become focused on the interior you. This interior you is a sanctuary of serenity. It is without the commotion and tumult whirling around in the exterior world. I am not asking you to dismiss the outside world as not real. I am not asking you to ignore it and pretend it doesn't exist. What I am asking you to do is become aware of the difference between what is going on around you and what is happening inside you.

There is a huge difference. The inside is always empty, always without variation. It is your mind that thrashes the inside with information. The inside offers no resistance. It allows for anything to come into it.

The point of all the above ideas is to help you gain entry to your inner self without carrying a speeding train weighed down by ten thousand screaming things from the outside world. You cannot change the outside with all its bombardment. It is what it is. What most people have failed to realize is that the inside is always at peace, if you can learn how to enter it. The inside is always undismayed, beyond the reaches of the most screeching sounds and chaos.

This truth is hard to grasp at first, but it will come to you with certain practices. If you want inner, lasting peace you must take charge of your life by recognizing you have been influenced deeply by the outside world. It has coiled itself around you like a boa constrictor. It has also infiltrated your mind, bouncing thoughts and images all over the neurons sending signals to your consciousness. You, and ninety nine percent of the people on Earth, have been split by the activities of the world from the sanctuary of serenity inside you that is untouched by the exterior stimuli.

The inside is your refuge away from the world. It is not an escape. It is a place where you recharge yourself to find a refreshing equanimity. This is your special room in your home where peace always resides. Go there by relaxing, breathing and telling your mind to wait outside the door because you need a break from it. It will obey you if you don't fight it. Gently ask it to go to sleep while you remain awake in the chamber of peace. This is the place you can always go to feel uplifted, to feel guided and nurtured by peace. This is the place that goes with you everywhere. You can find it easily in all situations. Even during a dire predicament, you can return to the chamber of peace inside you.

You can watch the outside world float past you, and you can witness the most shocking things unfold before you, and still remain in the center of your peace. No one will even know what you have done. You will not be a passive person unfazed by what is happening around you. You will actually see it clearer and from a place of consciousness so you can make sagacious decisions how to respond to it. You will feel peaceful no matter how trying the situation and how demanding it is because you will not push against it. You will not be trampled by it; you will not become a victim to it. You will stand in the midst of the storm with your inner peace giving you the strength to continue on in your quest of the sacred and the profound.

56.

Is There A Vengeful God?

The only vengeful God is the one we foster inside our twisted beliefs that are riddled with fear and unresolved anger.

The only vengeful God is the one that lives toxically in your head. In the past, religions and social systems invented the concept of a vengeful God as a means to control people with the ultimate scare factor. "The powers of creation will abscond with your soul by punishing you for the sins you commit." This was an effective measure to keep people on the good side of the societal mores. "A vengeful God will crush all violators." This is not only absurd, but is a dangerous indoctrination process that instills a small dosage of mental damage upon the part of the collective mindset of the people under this regime. It is toxic, leading to both punitive and horrific justification of forms of punishment.

Most people who believe in a vengeful God are operating under an obfuscated veil of fear. This fear leads to rigidity, intractability and paranoia. At its worse, it has permitted individuals belonging to large groups to support burning millions of people to death based upon ridiculous accusations of witchcraft and other distortions of life. Vengeance is an aberrant form of human rage that singles out its victims by unleashing brutal acts to right the wrong doing.

The cure for this negative, harmful and poisonous modality of thinking is to ask yourself these series of questions: "Would a God or supreme deity who created the stars and the Earth be endowed with the capacity to be vengeful? Would this God feel powerless as to possess a consciousness of retribution against one of the species it created? Does vengeance seem a likely characteristic of the creative forces of life itself? Has this God truly served humanity by offering love, joy and harmony?"

It is a powerful journey you have to go through to excise the layers of conditioning pounded into your psyche by a lifetime of overt manipulations. Peel them away! Throw off the shackles of thousands of years of systems demanding your conformity until you stand unencumbered so you can invent the identity best matching the spirit gliding through the world as you.

57.

How Can We Live More In Present Time?

When we can trust the world and trust ourselves, we can be fully alive in present time.

This is a great question because it is the crux of how most of us operate as we traverse the paths of our life. The human mind is a fantastic tool benefiting us immeasurably. It brings past memories along with it so we don't fall prey to the pain of the mistakes we made in our earlier days; it also keeps us ever alert about an unformed future, enhancing our chances of successfully surviving. In other words, the mind serves us by offering energies not of the present time. This is not always in our best interest. This form of existence drains us of our enthusiasm for the present time.

Children live purely in the now. This is why they are generally so happy. Haunting feelings of the past or insecurities about the future do not beleaguer children. We are charged by a frisson of emotions lying underneath the surface that keeps pumping blood to our fear mechanism.

The main ingredient needed to allow the present to happen more palpably and consciously is trust. It is not about trusting the world around us. This is a huge fallacy for most of us. What we need to do is trust ourselves. We need to trust we will be safe without having to succumb to the extreme vigilant thought patterns running rampantly through our heads. We need to trust in the forces from which we were created, that they are fundamentally designed to keep us floating as we sail down the river of our destiny.

Trust is not about controlling our lives—although most people think it is. Trust is about letting go of control and feeling safe in the unknown of the Universe. Don't use a set of religious belief systems to act as a crutch you lean on to make you feel safe. Let go of everything. Say to yourself, "I am a part of the grandeur of the Cosmos. It created me. Whatever happens is beyond my control. But I trust in Creation to guide me successfully into the next moment."

Living in the moment is pure freedom. It is a pervasive relaxation engendering a deep, sweet, nurturing sense of peace. Live in the moment by allowing yourself the glorious gift of enjoying whatever has been proffered by life for you to discover, to learn from, and to enjoy by surrendering to the highest power there is: the miracle of the moment!

58.

When Will Humanity Live In Peace And Joy?

When we stop seeing another person as an enemy, we can cross the chasm of separation to begin healing the fallacy of division and exclusion.

It seems our genetic predisposition is to invite and seek out conflict within the self and with others. We live in juxtaposition with others who have dissimilar views, values and lifestyles. This sets the stage for problems, both small and large. We have never been a species fostering peace and harmony among ourselves or with other species cohabitating the Earth with us. We have always been at war, to varying degrees, with everything around us.

The skills needed to learn how to reconcile conflicts elude most of us. These skills are paramount in order to heal. Logically, harmony is a far better state of feeling than friction. Harmony not only feels better, it helps us to improve the conditions of our lives. Society becomes the beneficiary of harmony. Everything we touch and contact benefits from an intrinsic state of harmony. Yet, pathetically, we have never achieved harmony collectively. We are defective in cultivating harmony as a society.

How do we create this appealing way of being? How do we all mutually agree upon an unbreakable commitment to becoming harmonious creatures living in the inescapable mystery of the planet Earth?

We can't do this as a group, unfortunately. We cannot expect all seven plus billion people alive today to adhere to the same formula promoting harmony, peace and joy. This cannot be achieved without some unimaginable miracle. But what we can do is rearrange our own personal life to become our ideal self. We can do this by our own free will to choose how we want to live and how we want to interact with others. It can be done on a personal level with relative ease— if you are truly devoted to altering parts of your life.

There are many steps necessary to start the process of transformation. One is to accept the truth that there have been turmoil, anger, fear, worry, jealousy, condemnation and hatred living inside you throughout your life. And, at times, these characteristics have been unleashed with a furious discharge of emotions. It is also vital to neither deny nor repress these feelings. They cannot be excised from the complex makeup of a human being. They will continue to live inside you.

But what you can do by acknowledging them is to learn how to modulate these emotions so they do not control you. You can learn to take the reins of your destiny by choosing to be in charge how you think about outside events and how you react to them. When you choose to be a peacemaker, your body vibrates differently. Your entire being relaxes, trusting a higher order in the dynamics of relationships with others. When you choose to live in harmony, it becomes increasingly difficult for something on the outside to throw you off course!

This is an easy concept to accept, but the reality of applying it as a standard practice in your life is immensely difficult. It takes discipline. It takes passion to be in charge of your life. It takes a new set of beliefs empowering you on your journey to the stars. You must choose a new path to follow, one filled with mystery, beauty and peace. You cannot change the outside conditions of the world, but what you can do is decide in every moment how you will respond to these conditions.

Bring harmony as best you can to every situation. When you do this, you give a gift to yourself and to the world. Peace is synonymous with joy. It is impossible to be joyous when you are trapped in a state of disharmony. When you exude peace, you affect the other people around you. You can change dreariness to happiness just by the harmony emanating from you. The future of our survival may very well depend on how successful we are in making harmony the fundamental nature of who we are.

59.

What Are Your Thoughts About Heaven And Hell?

How we choose to live will determine if the experience is either a glorious adventure or a dismal struggle.

The concept of heaven and hell is a misleading one. There is no hell except in our minds. The idea of heaven after we die has been used to dangle a sweet candy promise to the living to keep them behaving within the accepted boundaries of their society. When we die there is only perfection—no punishing God to ship us off to hell. While we live, there is a heaven within us but we must coax it to the surface of our experiences by endowing it with our vitality, truth and passion.

We are the architects of heaven on Earth. No set of conditions can preempt this fact. Nothing can tear our love of life from us unless we allow it. Hell is when we play victim to outside events and conditions. Then we suffer, wail, denounce, and crawl through life as if our legs were too weak to carry us.

Use heaven and hell as a metaphor for how you want to live in the moment. Do you see beauty all around you, or do you wallow in misery because you didn't get your way or whatever? One animates your being with an experience of a heaven-like thrill. The other thrashes your experience as though someone threw mud all over you and you feel horrible, caught in a hell-like grip! The choice is always yours. You are always the master of your experiences, always in control of your responses to anything. (Though many people feel this is not the case.)

Some people will say there are horrific situations where it is impossible to feel you are in heaven. Yes, there are moments when your world momentarily collapses with an eruption of hot lava engulfing you. You can't ignore these times. What I am saying is to use the inner light of your soul to find the heaven in your experiences as often as you can. This is the meaning of heaven and hell. They are not places existing in an afterlife. They are the conditions of your mind and feelings of how you want to create a life for yourself. Choose hell and suffer. Choose heaven and thrive. It's a pretty simple choice. Now be the master of the one you want to embrace!

60.

How Does One Best Handle The Death Of A Loved One?

Mourning is a profound journey that cannot be rushed or ignored.

Weep. The loss of a beloved is inconsolable. When a loved one is taken away forever by death, a pain of despair and emptiness pierces the heart. There is nothing to do except to feel the grief.

You can relive the memories of the person who has died. You can also cherish the life of the deceased by taking one or several of the best attributes of this person, applying them to your own life. You can carry the love in your heart with you for the rest of your days. And you can know on some deep, mysterious level that your loved one's soul is still connected to you.

Give yourself time to heal. Never rush the mourning process. The anguish will never fully be gone. Yet you will, in time, grow to appreciate your own life to a greater degree. You will find magic in the smallest things. A shaft of sunlight in the morning coming through a window. The chirping of a songbird. The fragrance of a jasmine flower. The piano notes of a favorite song. In these things you will feel the love of your beloved reminding you to find the sacred in everything. And you will know a peace abiding in your soul for which there are no words.

61.

How Can People Show More Compassion?

*The more compassion you have for yourself
and every other living thing, the closer you
will get to what is called Divinity.*

C ompassion is the most important part of human
life that can produce a world where everyone
benefits. The lack of compassion is the essence
of the world's woes. Without a healthy level of compassion
for you and for others, including animals and the Earth
itself, life becomes a burden and a chore. Nothing is
more important than to hold compassion in your heart
and to act upon it as the touchstone to how you live.

The first thing to explore is what is compassion?
It is when you care for something so deeply your

only focus is to see it reach an exalted state of being. Compassion is honoring and valuing every expression of life. Each person and every animal is a sacred creation of the Universe and needs to be cherished. You give altruistically to empower another person or animal. You behold everyone with love, trying your best to make life a joyous and fulfilling experience—without needing credit in return. Compassion is being a steward to the endless array of life on the glorious planet Earth! It also means you treat yourself kindly and reverentially.

Why is compassion missing from the human experience? There are many reasons. One of them is when a person is so caught up in his survival he cannot think about someone else. People also view outsiders as strangers who do not belong to the same family. Outsiders are seen with suspicion and distrust. We go around the world with a covert hostility toward people whom we do not know because we fear they may hurt us or take away what we have achieved for ourselves.

Compassion is a force contained in the human soul that, when displayed, is one of the most spectacular expressions of creation in the Universe. When we can give unconditionally to another person or animal, we are reaching the highest level of aiding in the future survival of life itself! Make a concerted effort to be compassionate every day of your life. Ask yourself if your actions are doing everything possible to bring the experience of joy to those around you. Nothing is more precious and more rewarding than an act of compassion!

62.

Why Are Some People Staunch Atheists?

No one knows the nature of the Universe or its purpose so we must be careful to not be too presumptuous with our conclusions.

We humans have a little voice inside our heads that keeps telling us we need to be in charge of our lives. We need to think we know answers to the smallest and the most mysterious things about the nature of the Universe. Wanting to know, wanting to study and examine things is a healthy, positive path to follow. But for the person who proclaims to understand the nature of things, there is a huge missing component.

The mind cannot grasp things beyond its limited capacity. Many atheists are coming from a reactive point of view from the truncheon blows of traditional religions in history whose hypocrisy and retributions left bloodshed, grief, and horrors in their wakes. I understand the cause of this form of denouncing the existence of God. I understand the indignation the atheist must feel in his heart and soul.

However, the atheist is drawing injudicious conclusions about God in order to manage his life in a linear, practical manner. God is not some anthropomorphic deity sitting in the clouds casting judgment over the lot of humanity based upon its ability to live magnanimously or under the yoke of moral turpitude. All forms of describing God with human characteristics are merely narcissistic and absurd!

In truth, there are no atheists if you use the logic they apply to come to their conclusions. Let's dispense with semantics because I believe the word God and its connotations are what fuels the energy firing the atheist's mind. Call God whatever you want. Call it Nature! Call it the unknown. Call it the mystery of how things happen to come together. Call it just something that is beyond human comprehension. Whenever a person thinks about the cosmic forces that created the physical Universe, he is describing God. This God may not fit the orthodox concept of God, but even the most ardent atheist will agree there was some form of natural phenomenon responsible for our existence. If you don't believe in God, you still believe life happens on Earth. This is sufficient reason to remain in absolute wonder without a single clue what the truth is. Call this God.

63.

What Are Humanity's Greatest Achievements?

Everything we do is an achievement in gaining mastery over limitation and ignorance.

Our greatest achievements are so immense in scope it is impossible to elucidate or list them. Let me list just a few of them. Let's start with language, the spoken word. What an extraordinary achievement this is by itself. Add to that the written word and you have pure magic! We have been able to manifest many of our wildest dreams by sharing our thoughts with others through verbal and written communication. Coming together in small groups and then developing agriculture was in itself a miracle, which gave us the needed ingredient to survive for thousands more years. Transportation—the wheel, roads, and then boats to transport our goods from one location to the next—is an amazing achievement.

Educating people was the touchstone birthing a new world for humans. With our skills, we learned to build unimaginably fantastic structures such as houses, temples, mausoleums, entertainment centers, factories, and museums. Architecture became the collective will of humanity to take the Earth's elements and shape them into buildings where we could flourish. Art is one of our greatest achievements because it helped inspire the creative part of our brain so we could better understand life and death.

Our desire to explore the world was another achievement setting the stage for our growth and advancement. The cultures we discovered gave us a plethora of new ideas to help with our survival. Slowly, over centuries, these ideas spawned the inventions of technology, space travel, movies, television, the web, and medical marvels saving and prolonging millions of individual lives!

One of our greatest achievements we have made is our ability to think and to understand our nature. With this we have been able to uncover the secrets of who we are. We have been able to probe into anything with an unwavering resolve to discover its essence. All this thinking has enabled us to unmask the primordial fears and superstitions keeping us trapped so we can know the unfettered, magnificent miracle of a life bursting with freedom, joy, beauty and love!

64.

How Does One Become
More Spiritual And
Access The Divine?

*The more love we can offer freely to each
moment, the more our lives become divine.*

othing is more sacred than when you embrace
every facet of life as manifestation of spirit.
When you behold every unfolding event as
an expression of the oneness of all life, you will have
reached the highest level of consciousness. Stop
seeking; cease striving; end the need to find spiritual
truths. Truths are coming in abundant waves washing
over you in every second. Become aware of them.

Open your eyes to the spirit inherent in all things.
Never separate yourself from divinity. It lives in every

fiber of your being and in every fiber of both animate and inanimate objects. The grass is spiritual; the wind is spiritual; the mouse is spiritual; the pebble is spiritual; your dreams and your words and your life are spiritual. Know this and you will live in a perpetual state of sacredness. In every fiber and atom in the world lives the divine. The nature of creation, with its myriad expressions, is divinity. There is magic, power, beauty, and wonder inherent in everything!

65.

Are There Hidden, Esoteric Forces Shaping Our Lives?

We shouldn't impose our beliefs on to the world because what we know is merely an extension of our experiences and not the experiences of other beings.

This world is so mysterious our minds cannot begin to imagine what is behind the physical plane. We grasp things in the three dimensional realms. There are energies happening simultaneously about which we have no idea. Intuition taps into one of them. Our prescient ability is also another form of gaining access to the nonphysical world. Although many individuals take advantage of the gullibility of others by exploiting them, there are seers, mystics and clairvoyants who have an uncanny ability to cross over from the material world to the nonmaterial world.

No one can explicate or verify the existence of these metaphysical phenomena by the standards we use to measure our world. But they do exist for sure. How they shape our lives and what specific influence they have on us is probably greater than we realize.

This is why it is important to align your energy and your consciousness with the highest place of light. Live by the highest values; live impeccably; open your heart wide to the grandeur of the world. Be aware of your emotions, for in them you can feel small pieces of the other reality. Remember your dreams, for they too offer glimpses of the powers beyond the physical place. Everything we know is like the wind circling the Earth. We feel it and are influenced by it, but we don't know its origin and where it started or ends. Life is also like the mist of an ocean—something we see and feel, but cannot understand its essence.

66.

What Does It Mean
To Have Freedom?

Freedom is not based upon outside conditions because its true nature begins within each of us.

Everyone has his and her freedom all the time. Freedom is omnipresent even when you are incarcerated or caught in a tight predicament. The reason I say this is because true freedom is not about an external set of circumstances. Freedom is an inside affair. No one can steal your thoughts, feelings or dreams. These are the sails catching the winds of freedom. You are the architect of your destiny. You can turn any moment into a shrine and a blessing, or you can act like a thief robbing yourself of all your beauty

225

and joy. Freedom is about making the choice to live as you desire and in the fashion matching your soul.

Most people look at the physical conditions of their lives in deciding if they are free or if they are enslaved. Look deeper. Yes, the conditions around you cannot be ignored, nor should you treat them perfunctorily, for they impact you and your ability to be autonomous. This can present challenges for sure. Sometimes the situation you find yourself caught up in can feel oppressive with no way out.

At the same time, the greatest freedom lives within you and cannot be trapped by outside events—unless you allow them to do this. The mind is a fertile ground sprouting living things in the forms of thoughts and ideas. This is the greatest freedom in the world simply because it defies being conquered by an outside intruder. You alone are in charge of the mind within you. Therefore, you are the sovereign master of the life you have been bequeathed by the powers of the Cosmos.

67.

How Do We Know When We Have Found Enlightenment?

We are all on an endless journey of discovery, which has no end.

Finding enlightenment as a destination is a fallacy. There is no enlightenment to reach or find. Learning is a never-ending process. Wisdom comes from direct experiences, and these never stop until the day you die. There is no moment in anyone's evolution where enlightenment is found. Too much searching and striving can become a detriment to hastening growth. Don't push so hard. Relax and trust in the process. Thinking too much is a form of slavery. It becomes a trap feeding the ego. Then your

227

knowledge and discoveries lead to self-aggrandizement. Be your authentic self; be natural; be peaceful; be playful; be inquisitive; be spontaneous and creative.

Enlightenment is shedding light upon yourself. It is awakening from the slumber of fear and apprehension, discovering the joy of life. It is unhinging your mind from the bondage of fear so that your awareness is not constricted by illusory limitations.

Enlightenment is when you dance without tiring; when your love does not discriminate; when you behold all beings as miracles created by a divine plan; when you sit down to pay homage to a sunset and know you have never left the perfection of life.

68.

What Is God?

God is something we create based upon how
we want to perceive the world.

Since the beginning of human development, people have ascribed characteristics to God reflecting the conditions of the times. All of these characteristics have some elements of human attributes to them. We are too presumptuous in thinking we have an understanding about the nature of creation. We do not.

God is creation. It is the force, thing, and energy behind everything. It has always been there—even before the birth of the Universe. It is the space between atoms. It is a swan and a snake. It is a rock and a drop of water. It is the planets and the celestial bodies. It is gravity and black holes. It is time and nothingness. It is zillions of Universes. It is life and it is death. God is your eyes, your thoughts, your dreams and your fears! You are God presiding over your life. No one thing in all existence can be separated from God.

The religious concept about a heavenly supreme being, omnipotent master of all things, was summoned by the human need to feel safe and secure in a totally unknowable existence. This gives us a glimmer of faith and security to allay the fierce insecurity lurking in our cells. We created this idea of a judgmental God to answer questions that are unanswerable.

Yet the truth is that God is the essence and expression of every infinitesimal thing that is seen and unseen. God is the spark, the flame, and the creator of the imponderable mix of everything giving us substance and animating us with energy. God is magic and mystery and wonder and amazement. By profoundly cherishing everything around us, we can begin to grasp the nature of God.

69.

What Is Death?

We know so little about life how can we expect to know the secrets of death?

Death is the ultimate mysterious frontier. Everything has a cycle of finite time in which to exist—a tree, a rock, a person, the Earth, and the galaxies. We are all designed with a predetermined time frame. Nothing can elude the inevitability of death. This truth has shaken us our core, leaving us so shocked we have created wild, beguiling, fanciful and extraordinary stories about the nature of death.

Death is another portal through which all things pass. It is a final sunset of who we are in the present form. Whatever happens to us when death comes will be as much of a surprise as was being squeezed out of the womb

231

at the beginning of our lives. The physical properties of the known Universe are constantly in motion, changing and going through amazing transformations. Nothing can be destroyed; things morph into something different. I suspect this is the case with the atoms of our dead bodies. We will be scattered and then reshaped into something unimaginably miraculous. Perhaps we will join a star and burn for billions of years as intense light until we explode into something totally new.

Spirit is the power and energy of creation living everywhere inside our bodies. Since spirit is not of matter, it continues on after we have discarded the body. This journey is eternal. The actuality of it can only be experienced once we die. It should be a wild ride unlike anything we can imagine.

70.

What Is The True
Purpose Of Life?

*To be fully alive without fear and constraints
is to become one with the purpose of life.*

This is a proverbial question everyone asks over and over. The answer is simple. The purpose of life is to explore yourself to discover who you are. Once known, you live it with great passion, joy and reverence. One of the main purposes is to embrace your spiritual nature, finding peace in the refuge of your soul.

Once you awaken from the illusions of the world, you are free to celebrate the gift of life in every moment. Then you learn, you transcend, you rejoice, you love and you give ceaselessly to the world with immense gratitude and appreciation. You love from your heart, dancing and singing as you make your way down the amazing path of life!

SECTION FIVE

Other Subjects

There are many subjects in the world that elude our understanding. We all want to make sense of the world. Life can often be a conundrum that confuses us. In this section we enter into the realms of subjects for the sole purpose of greater breadth of knowledge. Knowledge is synonymous with freedom and joy. Nothing can be as sublime as feeling at the summit of freedom. This feeling brings us closer to our love affair with life.

71.

How Can The Disparate Cultures, Religions and Nations Of The World Unite Peacefully and Respectfully?

When we learn that all tribes belong to the same planet, we will work together synergistically.

Throughout history problems have been widespread among the various cultures, religions and nations on Earth. Many people look askance at a different way of life. They hold biases and suspicions in their thoughts when looking at a different set of conditions than the ones they are accustomed to experiencing. Friction happens easily when differences collide. The heterogeneous groups flourishing in the world are often at odds with each other. It is one of the most challenging things we face as a species.

The first thing to examine is why is this so common? Where does this come from and why such viciousness toward something that is different? People are bred to be leery of things that do not match their own paradigms of behavior and beliefs. Newness intimidates many people. We have deep insecurities lurking within our psychological makeups. We fear losing what we have and we fear things we cannot understand or explain. This disease of the mind compromises our ability to coexist with other cultures harmoniously. It comes from thousands of years of marauders attacking and destroying. It comes from the memory of suffering at the hands of outsiders. It comes from an overzealousness to stop invasions on small or large scales.

The irony of xenophobia is that it hurts us more than it helps us. It actually weakens who we are because it narrows our scope of trust and understanding, forcing us into a trap where our minds become stale from astringent thinking. Disdain for another culture only shrinks our creative selves. It forces us into habits that, over time, become torpid and unproductive.

The truth is we all benefit when we embrace cultures that are different than the ones we know. We can learn more about the world when we are receptive to varying life styles. People from other nations have a separate history than we do and the more we can be open to these people, the broader our understanding of life becomes. Instead of fearing these people or blocking out what they have to share and what they believe, we should open ourselves to them to receive a new perspective illuminating who we are.

We all belong to the single planet sustaining us. We all came from the same set of physical and chemical conditions creating life. We are all a singular point of existence with slight variations. The more we embrace each other, the more unified and glorious life becomes.

Religions for the most part maintain dogmatic positions, fostering a network of accepted beliefs and rituals. When a person deviates from these beliefs, the religion is threatened and assumes a defensive position, often rejecting the person who questions its absolute authority. Religions desperately need to embrace other spiritual organizations with kindness and reverence. They need to reverse exclusion by turning it into inclusion. It's fine for a religion to have its own rituals and beliefs. But what is not fine and leads to consequences of separation and possible conflicts is when a religion proclaims supremacy over others; when it denounces other belief systems as invalid; when it promotes hostility by disrespecting other religions.

It is time in our evolution as a species to change the tenor of our beliefs as spiritual beings to include everyone else in the world—as long as they embrace a healthy and vital set of beliefs screaming gloriously for a better quality of life for everyone!

72.

When The World Teems With Beauty, Why Aren't There More Poets And Artists?

Each of us is capable of reaching enormous heights of creativity.

To leap out of superficial trenches takes courage and inspiration. To taste the delicious, raw flavors of the world means you are willing to consume new fruits abounding in the garden of life. Lying dormant in every person is the secret of the Ages. A sleeping mystic lives within us all. We have just been bewitched by a spell of fear that drained us of our adventurous nature.

We are all tumbling through the mystery of existence. We are all poets, guardians of life's secrets. Some of us write

different verses by the way we move through the world—
voluminous anthologies; cryptic sonnets; luminous lyrics
and refreshing revelations. We all leave legacies of truth
in glowing triumph in parades of grand celebration!

73.

What Are Your
Perceptions Of Children?

*Every child comes into this world with an
unmarred set of conditions.*

C hildren are unformed, innocent, pure beings who
naturally gravitate to positive energy. They are
angels awakened to the dream of life. They are
basically free of any leftover conflicts from any previous
incarnations, if such things truly exist. The reason we
are so enchanted with children is they have no pretense,
no hidden motives. They express themselves naturally, in
the moment, fully alive and present to what's happening
around them. Their emotions are transparent, pure,

unfiltered. Adults feel refreshed around children because they love unconditionally. All you have to do is love them.

Children make us feel young again because they frolic in the moment. Happiness is their natural state. Play and laughter spring forth from them spontaneously. We can learn from children by listening with our hearts to what they say and to what they do. They can be our best teachers. Follow them and you will find flashes of timeless wisdom in the innocence they display. Spend time with them and you will know the richest freedom in the world. Love them and you will merge with spirit. Children are little angels sent forth to remind us about our true nature.

74.

What Is Art And What
Is Its Function?

All art is an expression of the heart that
yearns to share a piece of the inner magic of
the artist.

All art is an attempt at explaining the mystery of
life from the human perspective without using
the standard methods of seeing something.
Art is beholding a slice of life by using a new lens of
imagination through which to study an object or life
form. Art makes us perceive our humanity without
the filters of our own thinking, looking from a different
vantage point into the essence of something. In this
way we can see its beauty, its whimsy and its magic
more clearly. Art is a reflection of the inner world of the

artist who has merged with a mystical power to capture a secret of creation in a momentary dance of truth.

Art is summoning the creative energies within the heart and soul of the artist. Through his or her bold and wild imagination, he reframes a sliver of the world by allowing us to glimpse the passion of the artist himself. Art is expressed in many forms. Poetry, painting, glass blowing, weaving, floral arrangement, sculpting, dancing, singing, film making and dozens of other modalities of art are bequeathed to us by the nobility, passion and imagination of the artists.

A child's first experience of creativity, whether it's scribbling on a piece of paper or playing with clay, is the irrepressible urge of the human spirit longing to discover some hidden secret behind the physical forms of life.

Art is a special language that takes the ordinary and unravels it to make it extraordinary. Art unveils its subject and then releases it for the rest of us to behold. Art is analogous to archeology in that it unearths things in hopes of finding the quintessential nature of its origins. This process also reshapes textures and colors and objects like refractions of light for us to see another layer of beauty. For beauty unto itself is one of the most hypnotic forces taming the restlessness of the human mind.

Another purpose of art is didactic because it may possess social and psychological ramifications, leaving powerful messages in subtle or overt forms for us to ponder and glean some truth that will slightly alter our lives. Art is one of the most evocative social instigators in existence. One of the amazing facts about art is it transcends cultural or national milieus. Anyone from any tribe on Earth can find things to appreciate about an art piece from a distant land.

Art is a link to higher consciousness; it is a portal into the mystery and grandeur of existence. The more receptive a person is to art the more he or she can witness things too profound for words.

75.

Why Do Many People Refuse To Vote For Important Political Elections?

It is the responsibility of each of us to contribute to the systems that govern our world.

It is true: a significant portion of eligible voters in many nations does not vote for a candidate in major elections. The reason people do not vote covers a wide spectrum. Most people choose not to vote because they do not feel an affinity with the eligible candidates. They do not like the choices and thus withdraw from participating in the election. There is another factor needing to be mentioned: apathy. Many people who refuse to vote do not care to engage in a system they feel is fundamentally corrupt and flawed. They are also absorbed in their own affairs, dismissing the larger political arena.

Another important reason people don't vote is they think their single vote will not matter. They rationalize not voting because they feel powerless to produce the desired results they would like to see happen. In some sense, they feel a modicum of power by not participating in a huge system where their individual involvement appears to be meaningless. Previous frustrations at failing to get their candidate elected have also discouraged people from voting.

With all this said, there is a missing component of vital importance. Every vote not acted upon is, in a sense, a vote for the opposing candidate. Most people who do not vote still have a slight preference among the available candidates. When a person selects not to vote at all, he or she is giving up the small contribution to a candidate who best fits the profile of the one desired. By not voting, a person is extinguishing the small flame of his power.

There are many people who would disagree with the above position. They would say they should not be coerced into voting for a candidate they cannot support. Voting for the sake of voting is not a valid reason to the person who does not possess a favorable attitude toward one of the competing candidates. Why should he compromise? Why should he be forced to cast a vote for someone he does not like? These are understandable reasons.

But then again, not voting is giving your power away to the sway of the masses. Not voting takes a person's participation and obliterates it. There is nothing to be gained by not voting, even if the person believes he is making an indirect statement by refusing to vote.

In a democratic society there is no perfect solution to the selection process of political aspirants. Every system has major flaws to its election process. These most likely cannot be fixed. But what can be done in a constructive manner is to make sure your vote—however small and inconsequential it may seem—gets registered as your voice to be heard and counted!

76.

Why Do Some People
Accept Mediocrity?

*A person escapes from the wild world when
fear rules his heart.*

Many people do not strive for a more exciting, adventurous, and daring life. They choose to proceed down the path of their lives in a sluggish, unchallenged manner. Mediocrity is the way of life for many people of the world. They do this because it is the easy path to follow. With a light load to carry, life becomes less complicated where there are fewer obstacles to surmount. Human nature gravitates toward the comfortable choice. There is nothing wrong with this attitude. There is nothing wrong with living a simple, serene, gentle existence where the person feels a beautiful sense of peace in his or her life. But there is a difference between a peaceful life and a mediocre one.

The mediocre one is when you hide behind your shield of apathy by remaining neutral about subjects, including your own life. It is when you do not take a strong stand for your beliefs and convictions, when you sit on the sidelines in an untenable state as you watch the parade of life gliding past you as if you were a spectator rather than a participant. A mediocre life is like volunteering to take a sedative daily that puts you half asleep so you won't have to feel the intensity of the world. It is when you wrap yourself in tape from head to toe and then try to dance. Mediocrity constricts the spirit within you from living the unbridled existence you were born to experience.

People follow the mediocre life for a variety of reasons. Mostly, they do it as avoidance so they won't have to face the frightening rawness of the challenges living within them as the world comes racing uncontrollably into their lives. It is a defensive position that cannot be defeated because, without keeping your feelings wide open, you are lulled into a sleep from which nothing can awaken you.

The solution to change the moment-to-moment state of mediocrity to one of powerful passion requires a willingness to love yourself for what lies beyond the surface. Most people have fears about what they may discover when they turn the light of scrutiny upon themselves. Be courageous and thrilled as you delve into the mystery of you. Be willing to adore the parts of you that have lain dormant for years, even the ones which seem repulsive, odious and not indicative of who you thought was the authentic you.

Embrace each part of yourself with all the love and passion you can muster. Bring these parts to the surface. Let them join you in the playground in the sun. Let them express themselves without your harsh critic condemning them because they make you feel self-conscious. When you own all parts of yourself, you will turn the life of mediocrity into one of splendiferous wonder.

You will celebrate the world and all its strange ways with every cell in you operating at its full capacity to feel, to think, to understand, to weep, to laugh, to love and to dream. You will dive into the waves of each moment without closing your eyes, without screaming in silence from fear. You will dive into the waves of life to become a part of them and to live in glorious rhythm with your soul. Each wave will wash away all the encrusted doubts that have burrowed into you over centuries. Then you will know the true meaning of the gift of life.

77.

What Are Your Thoughts About The Vegan Diet?

Eating healthy not only benefits you, but also benefits all the animals of the world.

There is probably no subject about which I feel stronger. I have spent much of my life learning about food and its impact on the body. I have experimented with various diets, some of which were extreme lifestyle changes. I am convinced that what we consume has a far greater impact on our health, constitution and longevity than most of us realize. The food we eat shapes us literally and energetically and spiritually. Ninety five percent of the people on this planet are either fundamentally clueless about food or don't believe it matters. (This includes dieticians and medical professionals.) The consciousness around food is abysmal. Neglect, disrespect and indifference rule the day for the majority of people on Earth.

Eating food laced with artificial ingredients, heavy pesticides and a slew of other human intrusions is akin to putting poison in our bodies. It is not the quantity of what we eat that is tantamount to health and vitality— it is what we eat. One of the most unaware things we do on a daily basis is invade our beautiful bodies with processed, fake, dead food. The consequences of this daily act are obesity, cancers, heart problems, high blood pressure, and a shortening of our lives.

I can't stand to look at a dead animal lying ripped to pieces on the road, let alone eat one that is cut into pieces, cooked and covered with spices! I have been a vegetarian for over forty years and a vegan for twenty years. Eating animals is not only unhealthy but also unnecessary for the vast majority of humans on the planet. Eating meat and seafood is not healthy. Do we really want to put the vibrations of a slaughtered animal's last moments of agony into our bodies? We harm the Earth by harvesting billions of chickens, lambs, fish, cows, and turkeys to eat. We cause horrific environmental damage to the seas, the land and the air by the processes needed to produce billions of pounds of dead flesh for us to devour.

In today's world, we have come far in creating a huge array of delicious, organic foods to consume. The taste of vegan food is magnificent! The food empowers you, is easy to digest, merges harmoniously with your body and serves the Earth as well. When the choices are vast in the vegan world, there is no excuse not to follow this wonderful lifestyle.

I believe future generations will look back at our carnivorous diet as barbaric as the way we view our early history when many of us were cannibals. They will also find that the consumption of flesh was directly responsible for many of our diseases and contributed to our aggressive dispositions.

I know much of this is upsetting to a carnivore. Most people don't want to give up their habits. They will use any excuse to continue eating meat. They rationalize why they have to eat meat: "The facts are inconclusive; we're all going to die anyway; how will we get our protein; other species eat each other; the vegan diet doesn't agree with my system; the American Medical Association doesn't endorse it; I feel hungry just eating fruits and vegetables." When people switch to the vegan diet they benefit themselves, the world and the other creatures sharing our Earth with us.

78.

How Do We Love Life?

The most natural and beautiful thing we can do is to cherish life with all its wonders and mystery.

You are here for a short time, probably less than a century. Your existence is a flash in cosmic time. Astounding biological and chemical phenomena created you out of the elements of the Universe. This unto itself is enough to send you flying into a state of rapture. If you were born with physical limitations or mental constrictions, you are still a stunning creation of Nature! You are the miracle called life. You can breathe, eat, see, talk, hear and feel the endless waves of the world racing through your body.

255

Life is a gift for you to experience and explore. With all its vicissitudes and challenges, with all its mysterious and inexplicable happenings, you are here to discover who and what you are.

How do you love life? Waking up is sufficient reason to love life. Every morning you have been given a new birth to set forth on an adventure throughout the day. Life created you, endowing you with certain features to interact with the forces of Nature. When you love this dream-like existence, you get closer to your spirit, the part of you that is mystical and deathless. When you love the world with all of its underpinnings and wild changes, you find yourself in a timeless place of wonder...like a child enthralled with the moment.

We humans often become bogged down with the mundane parts of survival and day-to-day living. Our perspectives become narrow and keep us hanging out on the surface of things, floating like driftwood in the tides. We take things for granted, especially our own lives. We lose contact with our deeper self. We forget what lives beneath the surface, the roots entangled endlessly with the great mystery of which we are an eternal part. We forget we are the components of the stars, a living entity of eons that shaped us inexorably to what we are today.

Loving this experience called you is the only route to take. Everything else is a self-inflicted punishment that is against the natural expression of life. Animals, plants, insects, and sea creatures do not lament about their lives. They probably do not even know what pity, misery and self-loathing are. We humans inflict our minds with dark thoughts uprooting our love of life. That's why we must use our thoughts to support us in our journey through this world. We must use our consciousness to remember the greater truth about our momentary life here on Earth. Whenever we think about who we should have been or what we could have done or why we were born into the conditions of our existence, we are diluting the purity and freedom to love life.

There is only one-way to love life. It is to take a deep breath of air, let it fill your lungs, and then let it go by releasing the need to change or control or to understand anything. Then feel throughout your entire body the energy of gratitude and appreciation you now own because you have realized in your mind you have landed here in this dream as a result of inconceivable powers who loved you enough to create you.

79.

Why Are Some People
Mean To Others?

Mean people are carrying within them an
arsenal of accumulated and unresolved
hurts from the past.

Rude behavior happens more often than most of us want to admit. Most of us dismiss these atrocious actions cavalierly. We say to ourselves the person is having a bad day or he is just hot-tempered. These people are not having a bad day. They are having a bad life. Buried inside them is an unhealed, vitriolic disdain for other people. People who display temper tantrums have been sitting on a keg of dynamite most of their lives. This may sound extreme, but it is not.

The truth is the people who spew vile words or actions at a moment's displeasure are fueled by a lifetime of blame, criticism and faultfinding that goes on in their heads multiple times throughout each day. These thoughts sink like dead weight into their bodies, remaining there as heavy arsenal, exploding at the slightest provocation.

They are angry to be inconvenienced by another person. It is a form of extreme egoism laced with some acidic hostility toward other people. Look into the eyes of these people who lose their tempers. What you will see is not just a burst of upset. Look deeper beyond the fleeting set of circumstances that has caused them to become unglued. You will see hatred lodged in their minds; you will see a broken person stewing in his or her own unresolved blame at the world for failing to appease him.

Throughout our lives most of us try to filter out the bad energy that enters our inner beings. We try to disarm these intruders by letting them dissolve before they begin to fester and grow into monsters inside us. The aggressive, hot-tempered person indulges his anger, thinking he can go around wielding his emotions without caring about the impact on someone else. This is why some people are mean to strangers.

The only way to transform this aberrant and socially destructive behavior is through a willingness of the person to plunge fully into an anger management program with other similar people. It will require massive attention and self-inquiry with the direction of a powerful facilitator. The anger is so deep-rooted and pervasive it will take months if not years to unravel the accumulated arsenal, replacing it with inner peace. You need to remember that the angry person has been operating his or her entire life under the regime of a tyrant.

To change the basic chemistry and personality of an inner tyrant will require an emotional transplant as complicated and all encompassing as a full heart transplant. The good news is this transplant could very well save his life before something terrible befalls him. The journey is a protracted one, but the rewards are spectacular freedom to live harmoniously not only with other people but with his inner self.

Once he has crossed the bridge from the bastion of darkness, he will find a road leading to a life brimming with wonder!

80.

What Is Your Idea Of A Utopian Society?

The main ingredient of a Utopian society is that everyone lives in harmony and peace.

My Utopian society would have many things in it to make it a wonderful place for every living member. The first thing it would have is peace. Rage and violence would be gone. People would respect each other, offering care and compassion to anyone when it is needed. All animals, fish, birds, reptiles, insects would be left alone to live in rhythm with their own destinies. The Earth, water, sky and every aspect of Nature would be revered where no harm would ever come to them. Children would be cherished and everyone would be given a great education. Housing would be plentiful with no one ever without a comfortable place to call home.

Technology would be used wisely and prudently. We would not be so dependent on technology for our happiness. Transportation would be designed with Nature in mind so we don't harm the resources of the Earth. Fossil fuels and other toxic forms of energy producing systems would be replaced with clean, safe, environmentally effective means to fulfill our basic needs. Building and construction would be kept in check; we would only build sustainable structures when absolutely required. The population of society would be under control and no one child would be brought into the world when the parents are not thrilled to have this child.

The military would no longer exist and weapons would be a dim blight on our memory. There would be no locks on doors, for stealing would not exist. People would feel safe wherever they traveled at any time of the day. Laughter and smiles would light up the faces of the people. There would be no strangers in this ideal society. Loneliness would not exist because individuals would always feel welcome wherever they went. People would talk to each other in meaningful, uplifting ways.

Kindness and gratitude would be the fundamental tenets of how people conducted themselves at all times.

Work would be a delight for everyone. Each person would find the career for which he or she was best suited. The conditions of work would be excellent. People would only work four or five hours a day, four days a week. The compensation would be fair and the highest paying member of society would never earn more than seven times the lowest paying person. There would be no unemployment; retirement would be when the person wished to stop working. Supervisors would be thoroughly trained, kind, respected leaders. The work world would flow smoothly and everyone would be financially stable and fulfilled.

Creativity would be the most honored expression of humanity. Theater would be loved; poetry would be cherished and revered by everyone; art would be like beholding a secret message created by a divine source; dance and music would spread across the society as a supreme beauty. New thoughts would be received with open minds. People would love to learn about new things. They would also love to experience many adventures. And most importantly, people would play all the time with each other—with love in their hearts and joy in their souls.

Spirituality would permeate the society—not as some structured system the people would be compelled to follow. Everyone's sense of the spectacular and the sublime would live in each moment in every material and nonmaterial thing. People would bless their own lives and the lives of everyone else. Visitors from other societies would be made to feel at home. Gratitude and appreciation would exude from everyone's hearts. Love would be the supreme manifestation of the way each person would live his life. Love for self; love for others; love for the day; love for the beasts; love for the mystery of life itself.

Sound ridiculously implausible? Well, at least we can strive to make some of these things become a reality. If we don't succeed, our chances of survival are weakened. Let's go for it!

81.

Why Are Many People Enamored With Gadgets And At The Same Time Alienated From Others?

We must remember that gadgets, although very useful, cannot provide us with love.

Technology aids us in our daily affairs. It facilitates the communication process and provides us with volumes of information. It is true our technology is racing ahead of our humanity. We are fascinated by the ever-changing technology around us. There is nothing inherently wrong with the amazing tools technology gives us. The problem is we have neglected the human side of things, giving priority to the machines. Technology needs to be incorporated into the human equation. It is a tricky thing to do because of the excitement and mass publicity the machine world blasts over the globe.

People get alienated from others in a whirlwind of the computer age because the heart has no place among machines. It is easy to forget your humanity when you are inundated by the slick gadgetry around you. You become disassociated from your feelings. You are lost in the whorl of machines that distracts you from examining and experiencing yourself. This is why people who are immersed in technology seem like androids with some vestiges of humanity. They have become disembodied from their own humanity. This is not healthy because they risk falling irreversibly into cyber space, never to return.

As a society, we need to consciously pull our heart and humanity along with the advent of new technologies. We need to place enormous emphasis on who we are and not get stuck losing ourselves in the machine world. Parents need to encourage their children to go outside to run in the meadows in spring and to play with other children—not with their devices. This will help them tap into their creativity and will also help them to learn about each other in natural social settings.

We also need to always remember who we are— living creatures that have evolved over millennia from tree-dwelling beings to the primates we are today. Yes, we are constantly evolving, but we need to make sure we don't try to circumvent important stages along the way by leaping into a futuristic nightmare when machines proclaim us as obsolete and do away with us because we are no longer needed.

82.

Why Is Music So Universally Loved?

Music is the enchantment of the heart allowing us to feel our emotions in their most pure expression.

Music is the language of the spirit of life, singing its rapture to us Earth beings. Music is the one creative force requiring no cognitive process to understand it. You don't have to think to get the wonderful audio vibrations of music. It takes the mystery of life and reshapes it into sublime sounds all of us can appreciate. It is so easy to receive you can even fall asleep listening to it and not miss a thing.

All other forms of artistic expression have roots in the culture from which they originated and require some prior understanding to grasp any meaning from them. This applies to literature; dancing; painting, etc. Music seems to me to have come from the heartbeat of the Universe itself, sending out waves of hypnotic sounds that flow right past our individual personalities, landing in the unified essence of the spirit of life itself.

Music is not intrusive nor does it demand our rapt attention. It instantaneously touches the inner cords of our sensitivity, making us feel good. It energizes us and propels our bodies to undulate in rhythm with the sounds. Music reminds us of the beauty of something beyond the ephemeral mystery of our own lives. It reminds us that all forms of life— past and present—are all connected by an invisible harmony not bound by time or by the physical world.

Music is the echo of eternity coming back to us over and over again.

83.

How Can I Become
A Better Writer?

Writing with passion and without restraint is
the only way to start the process of saying
something with meaning and depth.

The answer is relatively simple. Write from your heart. Write with passion. And most importantly, write for yourself. You can never succeed at getting people to understand you by using premeditated strategies you think will magnetically attract them to you. This will not work. Never write what you think others want to read. This is erroneous and is doomed to backfire.

Put punch in your writing by expressing the authentic voice that is yours alone in the world. Make your writing elegant like a proud peacock; make it sinewy like a ballet dancer; make it sensuous like swans in love. Write your truths with clarity, precision and vitality. By doing this, the content will sizzle with your truths; they will erupt like geysers whose spray will thrill you and teach you about the hidden dimensions of your own soul.

Love your writing as if every word were a child born out of the mystery of your soul. Writing is personal and magical. Never forget this. Make it descriptive and unique, using words and phrases that tantalize and seduce like the rapturous music of a great symphony playing its ecstasy for everyone to hear. Try to spin your writing with threads that weave a tapestry of exquisite beauty for you to behold. Never write to impress or to elicit a response from someone else. This kind of writing will invariably fizzle and leave the reader eager to exit from your work.

Writing is a deeply spiritual endeavor. Don't use trite and contrived phrases. Use words that say: "I am me! I am alive! This is who I am! This is what I feel! This is what I believe!" Remember, no one person and no authority can truly judge your writing. Writing is the creative expression of your soul, which no one person should demean because it is your essence unveiled before the world to be discovered and seen!

84.

What Are Your Insights Into The Fascination Many People Seem To Have About Wealthy And Famous People?

It is best we focus more on our lives and what we can achieve in our lifetime rather than obsessing over the life of a famous person.

People who experience their lives as drab and uneventful often find a vicarious thrill by living a fantasy life through a person with wealth and fame. We all get caught up in the excitement of a famous person's life because from the outside looking in, it seems glamorous, idyllic, and romantic. The famous person has something many of us covet: mass recognition. This appears to be very powerful to the anonymous man or woman living an ordinary life.

It is our nature to want acknowledgment. Somehow we think by having this lofty status we can escape the mundane lives we live. Somehow we think fame will make us invincible and all our needs will be met. Also, it is a far more pleasurable thing to dream about a famous person's life than it is to dwell on our own life that feels trapped on a treadmill getting us nowhere.

There is nothing wrong in taking an interest in famous people's lives. However, it becomes unhealthy when we endow our fascination with obsession. It would be far better for us to focus upon our own life, finding magic, beauty and value in who we are and how we can improve our lot in life. We should use some of the energy and time we spend reveling in the lives of famous people by developing and regaling our own creativity. Just because someone has wealth and fame does not make this person a virtuous, kind, creative, caring and happy person. We need to remember to look more closely at what is compelling us to think and act the way we do. When we can scrutinize our motives more precisely, we will sort out the refuse of our own low self-worth so we can find the gems hidden in the caverns of our souls.

85.

Since History Seems To Repeat Itself, What Will The Future Be Like?

The more we can develop our consciousness with positive values, the more likely the future will be a great place.

History never repeats itself. Our evolution has been so dramatically varied it's hard to believe humans of fifty thousand years ago were the same species as we are today. Think about how much has changed in the last twenty thousand years. We were hunters, nomads, wandering in endless search of prey and food. We were animals without societies, without wheels, without agriculture, without words and a million other things comprising our world today.

Look how much has changed in the twentieth century alone. It's staggering. Flight, radio, television, film, computers, space travel all came about in a matter of decades! Our civilizations change with great rapidity. And we change too. Our values, our ways of seeing life, our beliefs, and our temperaments are always in flux, influenced by the enculturation process. Change demolishes the status quo and roars like an unstoppable energy into the future.

I see a future remarkably more advanced in technology than where we are at today. I see humanity benefitting from these technologies; health and longevity will be significantly improved. People will get along better than today and will have more harmony with each other. I see people working together synergistically to build better cities; animals will be treated well and not killed for food; children will be cherished. Poverty, despair, hunger and many diseases will be minimal. Nations will work together, cooperating and sharing resources. Wealth will be distributed more equitably. The collective consciousness of humanity will be at a high level.

Women will have equality with men. All races will have full equality and animals will be cherished. We will be more attuned to Nature; the Earth will be treated with much care and respect. Everything will be done with grace and compassion. We will have made great strides spiritually. Humanity will work together to solve problems and to surmount obstacles. The quality of life will be exquisite.

Because of all these positive things, our bodies and minds will begin to change slowly over the eons. Don't forget who we were three to ten million years ago as early hominids. Millions of years before that we were tree dwelling mammals. Our bodies, millions of years in the future, will be very different. We will be stronger, quicker and more limber. We will be able to swim for miles; run for dozens of miles without stopping; leap thirty feet in the air.

We will be happy and fulfilled. Violence among us and toward other creatures will be gone. Laughter will come easily for all of us. We will play, sing, and dance in inspirational rituals as we celebrate life together. The need for leaders will be long gone. No one will be lonely or suffer the rejections of others. Competition will only exist in games where no one loses and no one gets hurt. Wild animals will have no fear of us because we glow with peace.

Seem impossible, far-fetched, and fantastical? What do you think humans ten thousand years ago would say if they suddenly landed in our world today? Tokyo, for instance? Las Vegas? Disneyworld?

Or inside the newest jet airliner? Seeing a patient getting a heart transplant or a cornea transplant from a cadaver? They'd all probably faint from shock.

Now let me add a million or two million years—a blink in geological time—to my future vision. Even my wildest images are prosaic when compared to the reality of what will be. If you have any doubt about such an idyllic future, you and I will be shocked when they come back to the twenty first century to ask us if we want to travel millions of years in the future in their time travel machine. The question I can't answer is: "Will we ever want to come back home to the twenty first century?"

86.

In The End, What Passionate Statement Would You Leave Behind For Others?

We have only one life in our present form and the more we can live freely and joyously, the more enriching our experiences will become.

You are a guest in the sacred house of life. You have been given this miraculous gift to experience the material world in this short journey through your body. You have been blessed by creation to be alive. Explore the house of life with much reverence. It is a hallowed and fragile house—teeming with wonders and mystery. Open your senses fully to the riotous magic spread before you. Love it wildly! Celebrate every moment! Rejoice in the glory of the world. Take nothing for granted.

Prostrate yourself before the altars of divine intelligence in animals, in trees, in flowers, in rivers, in clouds, in the faces of children, in the primordial cries of a trumpeter swan, in the colors of butterflies, in the dripping mosses, in the hot boiling pumice, in the memories of your own history and in the faces of people gliding past you like phantoms in a dream you have forgotten you are dreaming. For all of life is a dream of the Cosmos. And you are the center of the fire of life, blazing like hot embers, lighting the eternal firmament with your own unduplicated sparkle, panache and expression.

Walk the Earth in a trance of rapture. Make love to the air and to the rocks and mountains and impenetrable jungles. Run with the cheetahs; leap with the gazelles; dance with the winds! Unfurl your wings and fly! Fly to unexplored frontiers within yourself! There is so much to discover! The spirit within you energizes you. Fly to the stars!

And when it is time to rest and gather strength for the next day, surrender yourself to the deepest sleep you have ever known. Trust the unfolding mystery of the world. Be brave in the midst of inconceivable things; keep holding the torch of your faith. Higher! Higher! Let it rise above all desolation and mediocrity, for these are illusions in the house of life. Rise beyond the twisted fears of the small self and the entrapments of the dispossessed and the needy. But never scorn others; offer them your hand when the storm thrashes them. Remember, every man, woman, and child is your brother and your sister. They are your companions during your sojourn through life. Every beast, fish, bird and plant is a member of your family. Love each one in the silent ecstasy of your passion.

Carry only the possessions of your deepest dreams with you, the ones that need no luggage or crates. Carry them in your heart where they burn in glowing colors, reminding you of your mission in life. Never give up! You can stumble but never fall. You can weep but never turn away from the glowing light around the next bend. Carry the sweet memories of your life with you into the place spread before you without name. But never hold too tight to these memories, for they too will be released into the ethers of the unknown. Be like a child willing to leap into the next moment with unrestrained exuberance.

Believe in the impossible. Create the unimaginable. Stand taller than your highest principles. Shout your joy from the mightiest mountain. Shout your truths into the valleys where a thousand vanished civilizations once flourished! Tell them all who you are! Tell them everything you know. Tell them you know nothing. And laugh and laugh because you are so free nothing can fell the timbers of your mighty soul! Nothing can hold you down as you explode like thunder announcing your presence to the world.

You are the living manifestation of God's creation. Call God whatever you want. You are a pulsating force of the mysterious Universe. You were born out of the infinitesimal spark that gave birth in nanoseconds to the entire Universe! You are the child of the heavens. When you see another being you see the source of creation itself formed out of the mystery from which everything came. You are in everyone's soul. We are all astonishing pieces of the eternal oneness!

Neal Grace has always followed different paths to discover unexplored frontiers—from living in the woods for months, to traveling with a backpack around the world, to forging a career in the business world that gave him a taste of material comfort. A keen observer of the nuances of life, Neal began chronicling his experiences through the written word. He has performed at Grace Cathedral in San Francisco and other venues, sharing his passionate messages to inspire others to live freely and creatively. He believes the only way humanity can advance in its incredible evolution is for people to embrace the world with reverence and compassion. Neal lives in San Rafael, California with his wife Jacky.

INDEX

A

C

D

E

Earth 25, 59, 125, 144, 157, 160, 166, 171, 173, 175, 185, 195, 198, 203, 208, 212, 217, 219, 224, 231, 253–254, 257, 261–262, 268, 275, 279

early Earth 42
Earth's resources 172
lovely Earth 176
nations on Earth 235
planet Earth 183, 204, 213
save the Earth 170
tribe on Earth 245

Eclectic 152
Education 46, 146, 262
Elderly 142–143, 185
Elephants 144
Energized 83
Enlightenment 65, 227–228
Entertainment 115, 143, 182, 219
Enthusiastic 58
Esoteric 164, 187, 223
Evolved 137, 159–161, 266

F

Famous 272–273
Favorable 248
Fish 181, 253, 261, 280
Flaunting 141
Formidable 78

P

Panorama 43
Parents 36, 86, 91, 99–102, 119, 190, 262, 266
Passion 37, 53, 59, 65, 136, 205, 207, 233, 244,
    250–251, 270, 280
Peace 33, 57, 63, 74, 107, 147, 160, 163, 168, 182–
    183, 202–204, 206, 211, 233, 250, 261, 276
  inner peace 66, 193, 196, 260
  lasting peace 193, 195
  living in peace 145
  make peace 25, 97, 158
  peace with aging 162
  want peace 194
Peers 85, 147
People 23–27, 32–33, 36–39, 45, 47, 53, 58–65, 69,
    71, 73, 76, 79, 84–88, 92–93, 97, 101–102,
    105–106, 108–109, 111, 113–117, 119, 124–
    125, 128–133, 136, 140, 143–144, 146–147,
    150, 152–157, 162–163, 168, 171, 177–180,
    182–183, 188–189, 195, 197, 204, 206, 208,
    212–213, 215, 219, 229, 235–237, 247, 249–
    250, 252–253, 258–266, 270, 272–273, 275,
    279, 283
  afflicts people 31
  groups of people 122, 181
  *most people 28, 35, 41, 46, 49–52, 63–64, 68, 99,
    104, 151, 194, 198, 201, 226, 246–247, 251,
    254*
  people better connect 56
  people resist social changes 110
  problem with people 72
  schism between people 57
  spiritual people 53
  why don't people listen 68

W